ASPIRATION & DISSONANCE

READINGS IN HISTORY, RELIGION, AND GLOBAL AFFAIRS

JEFFREY LAMONICA

Kendall Hunt
publishing company

CONTENTS

INTRODUCTION

The world is, and has been, interconnected in many important and constantly changing ways. This presents us with opportunities and challenges as we seek our place in this global society. Facing these opportunities and challenges requires a comprehension of how political, economic, socio-cultural, historical, and environmental systems impact each other and affect human well-being. Human survival and advancement in the global context requires a balance between social equity, economic vitality, and ecological integrity. This publication aims to help students obtain a better understanding of the possibilities and contingencies we face in the broader world.

The world is also a diverse multicultural society. To better understand and coexist in this society, we must explore and understand the lives and experiences of historically marginalized people and the social structures that create this marginalization. Discrimination and privilege are based on a wide range of attributes including race, sexual orientation, gender, ethnicity, socio-economic status, religion, physical and mental ability, nationality, and immigrant/refugee status. Throughout this book, students will learn about the structures that enforce and perpetuate discriminatory systems of power and privilege and the social movements that directly challenge this inequity and discrimination.

Addressing the issues in this reader involves the cognitive processes of interpretation, analysis, evaluation, inference, and explanation. This critical reasoning requires certain dispositions of curiosity, a dedication to rational thought, a desire to seek out evidence, and a reflective awareness of one's own biases, limitations, and methods of inquiry. All of these skills will serve students well in all their academic and professional pursuits.

CHAPTER I

Ideology and Dissonance

Peasant Rebels?

Matthew Kowalski

> Of all the classes that stand face to face with bourgeoisie today, the proletariat alone is a really revolutionary class. The other classes decay and finally disappear in the face of modern industry: the proletariat is its special and essential product.
>
> —Karl Marx and Friedrich Engels, *The Communist Manifesto*, 1848

> For the preset upsurge of the peasant movement is a colossal event. In a very short time, in China's central, southern, and northern provinces several hundred million peasants will rise like a mighty storm, like a hurricane, a force so swift and violent that no power, however great, will be able to hold it back.
>
> —Mao Zedong, *Report on an Investigation of the Peasant Movement in Hunan*, 1928

INTRODUCTION

Marxism, in its many guises and forms, has unquestionably been both the most durable and complete critique of industrial capitalism. Central to the entire Marxist revolutionary project is the special, almost messianic, place of the global industrial working class (the Proletariat) as the only agent of historical change. As first outlined in *The Communist Manifesto*, orthodox Marxists have placed the proletariat at the center of their analysis.[1] Because of the working class's complete and utter alienation from productive forces, early Marxists conceived the proletariat as the only class capable of totally overturning society. Marx himself completely dismissed the peasantry as a reactionary force that was doomed to be consigned to the 'dustbin of history.'[2] As such, all traditional Marxists foresaw revolutionary upheavals occurring in those regions of the globe where industrial capitalism was at its most advanced and the traditional feudal peasantry had all become proletarianized. This would include western nations such as, Great Britain, Belgium, France, United States, and a united Germany after 1870.

The history of successful Marxist-inspired revolutions, however, significantly problematizes this traditional Marxist paradigm. Tsarist Russia, the first nation to experience a socialist seizure of power, was one of the most under-developed economies in Europe. The only successful European communist revolutions that followed in the wake of the Second World War, occurred in the predominantly peasant societies of Yugoslavia and Albania. If we extend our investigation further, to the colonial or developing world, then the central role of the peasantry in making and winning revolutions becomes even clearer.[3] Successful revolutions in Vietnam, Cambodia, Angola, Cuba, Nicaragua, Algeria, South Yemen, and most recently Nepal have all been built on the backs of the peasantry. Nowhere was this more apparent than during the long Chinese Revolution. Mao Zedong was the first Marxist thinker to truly conceive of the peasantry as the vanguard for the revolutionary change. For Mao and other non-western Marxists, the material conditions of colonial-developing societies necessitated a radical revision of Marxist orthodoxy concerning the revolutionary potential of the peasantry.

ORTHODOX MARXISM AND THE PEASANTRY

For all of its claims of universality, Marxism at its core began as a profoundly Eurocentric ideology. Both Karl Marx and Friedrich Engels conceived their theory of both history and revolution through the lens of 19th century European developments. This period witnessed massive socio-economic and cultural dislocations in western and parts of Central-Eastern Europe. Industrial capitalism and the unequal accumulation of wealth in the hands of a numerically small class of capitalists, created the necessary material conditions of class struggle. For all Marxists, the inherent contradictions of the capitalist mode of production would create the conditions for a new epoch of history. The 'vehicle of history' would lead mankind to a radically more equitable and free existence. In their view, all contradictions would eventually disappear into a borderless-classes utopia called Communism.[4]

The lone harbinger of the radical change was assigned to the industrial proletariat. This new

Statue of Karl Marx and Friedrich Engels

and rapidly growing class of laborers, who sold their labor power to the capitalist bour-geoisie, were viewed as the only socio-economic class capable of bringing about a total transformation of society. The proletariat's complete alienation from productive forces, as they were in a very real sense a commodity in the capitalist labor market, placed them outside of mature capitalism. Far from being beneficiaries of industrial moder-nity, the proletariat lost their autonomy as individuals. They would be consigned to an existence of robot-like slavery. Their very essence, life itself, was not their own. The proletariat, therefore, became in essence a class of industrial 'living dead,' with literally nothing to lose. Marx believed that as capitalism matured and expanded this class of 'industrial zombies' would grow in both size and desperation. Eventually critical mass would lead to the violent overthrow of existing capitalist society and the establishment of a socialist social-economic-political order, where the working class would control the modes and means of production. Thereby, restoring their humanity and paving the way for universal equality.[5]

Considering the importance Marx placed on the industrial working class in his con-ception of revolutionary change, it is not surprising that early Marxist writings took a very dim view of the traditional European peasantry. Orthodox Marxists saw the peas-antry as incapable of instigating and sustaining radical social change. While capable of mounting localized rebellions against the old feudal aristocracy and the increasing encroachment of capitalist modes of production in agriculture, these were in their view 'conservative' or backward looking uprising.[6] The aim of these peasant outbursts was not to create something radically new, but rather to turn the clock backwards. Peasant rebellions in Europe were largely concerned with the preservation of certain feudal privileges that were being erased by the wage labor economy and other features of rural life. In essence, the peasant was at best a 'conservative' rebel, only capable of localized bursts of spontaneous resistance or social banditry.[7] The localized nature of these peas-ant upsurges also prohibited the crystallization of a truly peasant class consciousness and any conception of solidarity with the predominantly urban proletariat. This is best expressed in Marx's classic *The Eighteenth of Brumaire of Louis Napoleon*, when he states . . . "The small peasants form a vast mass, the members of which live in similar conditions but without entering into manifold relations with one another. Their mode of production isolates them from one another, instead of bringing them into mutual intercourse. The isolation is increased by France's bad means of communication and by the poverty of the peasants. Their field of production, the small-holding, admits of no division of labor in its cultivation, no application of science, and, therefore, no mul-tiplicity of development, no diversity of talent, no wealth of social relationships. Each individual peasant family is almost self-sufficient; it itself directly produces the major part of its consumption and thus acquires its means of life more through exchange with nature than its intercourse with society . . . Insofar as millions of families live under economic conditions of existence that divide their mode of life, their interests and their culture from those of other classes, and put them in hostile contrast to the latter, they form a class. Insofar as there is merely a local interconnection among these small peasants, and the identity of their interests begets no unity, no national union, and no political organization, they do not form a class. They are consequently incapable of enforcing their class interest in their own names, whether through a parliament or through a convention. They cannot represent themselves, they must be represented."[8]

This lack of faith in the peasantry as a revolutionary class was coupled with a deep hostility on the part of revolutionary Marxists to peasant-based movements. As early as the mid-19th century, Marxists saw peasant protests as counter-revolutionary. During the 'June Days' of 1848, it was peasant conscripts that put down the Parisian workers uprising. Early Russian Marxists saw the failures of the agrarian socialist Narodniki of the 1870s, as largely being a byproduct of traditional peasant conservativism. In the words of Leszek Kolakowski, "No new Pugachev or Stenka Razin[9] made their appearance. Nor did the peasant reveal any latent enthusiasm for socialism; they were more likely to denounce the revolutionary agitators to the police than heed their appeals."[10] By the time of the Bolshevik Revolution and the Russian Civil War, despite Lenin's conception of a worker-peasant alliance, the revolutionary regime spent as much resources fighting a variety of anarcho-peasant bands as they did the Whites and foreign interventionists.[11] Indeed, this openly hostile attitude towards the peasantry was a defining feature of Soviet policy in the ensuing decades. The Stalinist Collectivization drive and subsequent 'terror famine' of the early 1930s was largely conceived as means of 'liquidating' the traditionally hostile peasantry through state-directed revolutionary violence transforming them into 'loyal' Soviet proletarians.[12]

MAO AND THE PARADIGM SHIFT

Whereas western Marxists viewed peasant insurrections with a mixture of suspicion and downright hostility, things were radically different in the revolutionary China of the early 20th century. An overwhelming majority of the Chinese population was (estimates range from 80%–90% at the time of the Boxer Rebellion) peasant. There was practically no industrial base nor for that matter either many workers or workers' organizations.[13] The little industry that did exist was largely foreign owned and confined to urban centers, such as Shanghai or Harbin, either on the coast or in Japanese dominated Manchuria. To be frank, from the perspective of an orthodox Marxist, China was quite simply not fertile ground for revolutionary change. Yet, it was from this seemingly unfertile soil that one of the last century's greatest revolutionary experiments sprang.

Owing to its largely agrarian economic base and the fact that it was essentially a semi-colony of Western colonial powers, Marxism came late to China. The Chinese Communist Party was founded in only 1919 and its modest membership was drawn almost exclusively from western-influenced Beijing intellectuals. Initially, following the advice of the Moscow based Comintern,[14] the movement allied itself with Sun Yat-Sen's

Portraits of Marx, Engels, Lenin, Stalin, and Mao

Guomindang in the anti-warlord and anti-imperialist First United Front. This alliance, however, was problematic from the start. While Sun and some others on the left-wing of Guomindang were intrigued about the modernizing potential of the Soviet experiment, they were never committed to the Marxist dream of utopian global revolution.[15] The Guomindang's right-wing, led by Sun's successor Chaing-Kai-seik, was openly hostile to Marxist ideas. This alliance of convenience unraveled in dramatic fashion in following the joint Guomindang-Communist army's liberation of Shanghai from local warlords in April 1927. After being informed that Chaing meant to betray them the Communists were urged on by both their Comintern advisors to launch a full-scale urban uprising. The local working class, although sufficiently radicalized, were outnumbered and out-gunned. The result of the uprising was the death of over 300–500 communist activists and perhaps over 5,000 Communist and Communist sympathizers being 'disappeared' as a result of the Guomindang's 'state terrorism.'[16]

For the young Mao Zedong and other activists who had escaped in the countryside, the 'April Events' only reinforced lessons they were already learning in China's agrarian interior. Far from behaving like counter-revolutionaries, the bulk of the peasants that the communists had organized into Peasant Associations in the areas they occupied, were taking the lead in the transformation and reordering of the countryside. It was the peasantry, with very little prodding by party cadres, that were redistributing wealth from and administering 'revolutionary justice' to local landlords. It was at precisely the moment of the failure of the urban-proletarian led uprising that Mao began to thoroughly challenge orthodox Marx principles concerning the agrarian classes and began a project that would led to a 'Sinification of Marxism.'[17] In essence, he was adapting Marxism to specific 'Chinese' conditions.

From Mao's perspective, this revision of orthodox Marxism was rooted in China's specific historical conditions. He was well aware that unlike the French or German peasants that Marx studied, the Chinese peasantry had supported the two massive revolutionary movements in the Taiping and Boxer Rebellions. The peasant-based Taiping movement, in particular, sought to achieve a truly radical break with the past and attempted to create a very literal 'Kingdom of Heaven' on earth.[18] This history of peasant support for utopian projects was coupled with Mao's acute reading of class structure in the Chinese countryside. Unlike Europe, the majority of Chinese peasants were classified as 'poor peasants.' These peasants were either "completely dispossessed of land and money or forced to sell their labor to either landlords or 'rich peasants.'"[19] They were a class of people with nothing to lose and everything to gain.

Mao's embrace of the peasantry was also based upon practical strategic realities. The 'April Events' in Shanghai had clearly demonstrated that an urban proletarian revolution on the model of the Paris Commune was simply not feasible in China. If socialism was to triumph in China, it would have to come about through a rurally based guerrilla struggle. This concept of 'People's War,'[20] later institutionalized as official military doctrine after the establishment of the Peoples' Republic of China in 1949, needed the support of the local rural population. The slogan was 'the people are the water and the revolutionary army is the fish; without the water the fish will die.' Only through good deeds and political work, would the guerrilla army gain mass support and be sustained by the agrarian population.[21] This strategy would prove to be the model for many of the successful modern revolutionary movements in the developing world.

CONCLUSION

A close examination of the evolving Marxist discourse on the revolutionary potential of the peasantry illuminates two major trends at play in Modern global history. Firstly, one must be mindful of the pitfalls of 'universalizing' narratives. The inherent Eurocentrism of orthodox Marxist thought proved inadequate in reading the socio-economic realities of the non-west. Secondly, the continued presence and durability of Marxist thought around the globe in the early 21st century would not be possible if the ideology was not fluid. Marxism, much like Christianity and Islam, continues to be relevant because it has been able to reinvent itself to meet a new historical epoch or cultural environment.[22]

QUESTIONS FOR FURTHER DISCUSSION

- For Marx and Engels, what is history? What forces or actors are important in their narrative of human development?

- How does mature capitalism sow the seeds of its own destruction? Why do Marx and Engels consider the industrial proletariat the 'only' revolutionary class? Why not the peasantry or the petti bourgeoisie (small capitalists)?

- Who is Mao addressing in this piece? Why is he writing this?

- How do Mao's observations about the situation in China clash with Marx's ideas about the revolutionary potential of the peasantry? What are the reasons he gives for his belief in the peasantry as an agent for societal change? Finally, what role does violence serve in both Marx and Mao's conception of revolution?

NOTES

1. Georg Lukacas, *What is Orthodox Marxism?* Marxism Internet Archive (1919) According to Lukacas, 'orthodoxy,' does not imply an uncritical view of Marxist texts. Rather, an adherence, to core texts.
2. Taylor, A. J. P. Introduction to *The Communist Manifesto* (London: Penguin Books, 1967), 25–26.
3. Consider Frantz Fanon's observation that "In colonial countries, the peasants alone, for they have nothing to lose and everything to gain. The starving peasant outside the class system is the first amongst the exploited to discover that only violence pays. For him there is no compromise." Franz Fanon, *The Wretched of the Earth*. (NY: Grove Press, 2004), 23.
4. See in particular G. A. Cohen's *Karl Marx's Theory of History* (Princeton: Princeton University Press, 1978).
5. This facet of Marxist thought is referred to as 'Accelerationism.' First elaborated in Marx's 1848 address, "On the Question of Free Trade," this theory has seen a surprising revival in recent years by a host of Neo-Marxist thinkers. In particular, see Antonio Negri, "Reflections on the Manifesto for an Accelerationist Politics." *E-Flux.* (2012).
6. See Eric Hobsbawm's excellent, yet dated *Primitive Rebels* (Manchester: Manchester University Press, 1959).

7. Hobsbawm, 12–23.

8. Karl Marx, *The Eighteenth of Brumaire of Louis Napoleon*. Marxist Internet Archive. (1852).

9. These were both leaders of rather sizable Early Modern serf rebellions. The majority of the Marxist historiography on these rebellions tends to fall-in with the 'primitive rebels' reading of these uprising. However, there exists a growing revisionist Marxist and Anarchist literature on these events that suggests a radically different reading. In particular see, Paul Arvich *Russian Rebels: 1600–1800* (NY: W.W. Norton, 1972).

10. Kolakowski, Leszek. *Main Currents of Marxism* (New York: W.W. Norton, 2005), 612.

11. See both Peter Arshinov, *The History of the Makhnovist Movement* (London: Freedom Press, 2005) and Eric C. Landis, *Bandits and Partisans: The Antonov Movement in the Russian Civil War* (Pittsburg: University of Pittsburgh Press, 2008).

12. See Moshe Lewin. *Russian Peasants and Soviet Power: a Study of Collectivization* (New York: W.W. Norton, 1968).

13. In fact, during the early stages of the Chinese Revolution, Anarchism proved to be the more popular western import for those seeking radical socio-economic change. See Maurice Mesisner, *Li Ta-Chao and the Origins of Chinese Marxism* (Cambridge: Harvard University Press, 1967) and Arif Dirlik, *Anarchism and the Chinese Revolution* (Berkley: University of California, Press, 1991).

14. This organization was an attempt by the new Bolshevik regime to reconstitute the Workingman's International of the pre-WW I period. It was intended as a forum for all of the Socialist-Communist parties that were influenced by the 1917 revolution. Also, the Comintern provided movements with funds, propaganda, weapons, and organizational expertise to these groups. However, by the early 1930s, the organization had thoroughly devolved into an extension of the Soviet foreign ministry and international intelligence services, such as the NKVD.

15. V. I. Lenin himself viewed Sun's 'socialism' with a degree of suspicion and thought of his movement as more of a populist modernizing/anti-colonial nationalist movement, like Kemal Ataturk's in Turkey. See V. I. Lenin, *Democracy and Narodism in China* (July 1912).

16. See Barbara Barnouin and Yu Chaggen. *Zhou Enlai: a Political Life* (Hong Kong: Chinese University of Hong Kong Press, 2006).

17. James DeFronzo, *Revolutions and Revolutionary Movements* (Boulder: Westview Press, 2011), 120.

18. See Jonathan Spence, *God's Chinese Son: The Taiping Heavenly Kingdom of Hong Xiuquan* (NY: W.W. Norton, 1996).

19. Mao Zedong, *Report on an Investigation of the Peasant Movement in Huanan* (March 1927).

20. See Mao Zedong, *On Guerrilla Warfare* (Urbana: University of Chicago Press, 1961) and Lin Biao, *Long Live the Victory of People's War!* Marxist Internet Archive (September 1965).

21. DeFronzo, *Revolutions and Revolutionary Movements*, 113.

22. Zizek, Slavoj. *Slavoj Zizek presents Mao on Theory and Contradiction* (London: Verso Books, 2007), 2–3.

BIBLIOGRAPHY/SUGGESTED READINGS

Hobsbawm, Eric. *Primitive Rebels: Studies in Archaic Forms of Social Movements in the 19th and 20th Centuries.* Manchester: Manchester University Press, 1959.

Kolakowski, Leszek. *Main Currents of Marxism.* NY: W.W. Norton, 2005.

Knight, Nick. *Rethinking Mao: Explorations in Mao Zedong's Thought.* London: Lexington Books, 2007.

Lowe, Donald. *The Function of 'China' in Marx, Lenin, and Mao.* Berkley: University of California Press, 1966.

Tucker, Robert. *The Marxian Revolutionary Idea.* NY: W.W. Norton, 1969.

Zizek, Slavoj. *Mao: On Practice and Contradiction.* London: Verso, 2007.

Emma Goldman: Radicalism and Feminism

Joseph Myers

> The history of the American kings of capital and authority is the history of repeated crimes, injustice, oppression, outrage, and abuse, all aiming at the suppression of individual liberties and the exploitation of the people. A vast country, rich enough to supply all her children with all possible comforts, and insure well-being to all, is in the hands of a few, while the nameless millions are at the mercy of ruthless wealth gatherers, unscrupulous lawmakers, and corrupt politicians.
>
> —Emma Goldman, *A New Declaration of Independence*, 1909

The idea of gender equality is perhaps even more difficult for people to agree upon than racial equality. Virtually no one who is discriminated against because of race believes their rights should be taken away, but there have been, and still exist today, many women who believe that they should hold an inferior status to men. Sometimes this belief in female inferiority is supported by religion and sometimes because of anatomical difference, but whatever the reason, women who have actively supported a woman's right to self-definition and self-determination have been seen as a particular threat in American society. Emma Goldman, 1869–1940, was one such woman. Goldman not only challenged the patriarchal standards of the Victorian Era in the late 19th and early 20th centuries, but she also challenged the power structure of the capitalistic democracy of the United States.

Regarding Goldman, United States Attorney Francis Caffey stated in 1918 that she was "a woman of great ability and of personal magnetism, and her powers of persuasion are such to make her an exceedingly dangerous woman."[1] But Goldman was not just any woman, she was a feminist activist, and she wasn't just any feminist activist, she was also an anarchist revolutionary. Dangerous to the system might be an understatement. President Theodore Roosevelt put it more directly when he stated in a presidential address in 1901 that Goldman represented "a crime against the whole human race."[2] What was her crime? Not merely advocating total political, social and economic freedom for all individuals through getting rid of any institutional government, but her real crime was being a woman who loudly spoke out against injustice at a time when women were supposed to maintain a subordination to men.

Emma Goldman immigrated to America as a teenager in 1885. Her family in the Russian Empire had fallen in and out of poverty, but they had been prosperous enough that Emma did receive schooling. In the year following her immigration to the United States a peaceful worker's demonstration in Chicago erupted in riot as police tried to clear demonstrators from Haymarket Square. The Haymarket Riot, as it has become known, resulted in the death of several demonstrators and police officers, and led to the conviction and execution of several anarchist speakers, who were not even in the square at the time of the riot. Goldman became interested in the anarchist cause of promoting freedom through total economic and political equality of individuals, and through getting rid of governing institutions that supported the power of economic elites.

Goldman first settled in Rochester, New York, where she became a factory worker. She also married and quickly divorced. Her life of activism began around 1888 when she left Rochester for New York City. There she began to associate with political radicals, and met Alexander Berkman, who would be her long-time companion. In 1892 Berkman, with the help of Goldman, devised a plan to assassinate the manager of a Carnegie steel mill in Homestead, Pennsylvania. The strikers did not invite Berkman, and

The Haymarket Riot in Chicago in 1886

were not in favor of radical ideologies like anarchism or socialism, but Berkman thought his efforts would aid in the cause of all workers in the fight against the inequality of the capitalist system. Leaving Goldman at their home in Worcester, Massachusetts, Berkman went to Homestead to martyr himself in the worker's cause. He shot Henry Frick, the steel mill President, but did not kill him, nor was Berkman himself killed. Instead he was captured and sent to jail. While Goldman

Emma Goldman and Alexander Berkman

never completely disavowed the use of violence to bring down what she believed to be an unjust system, most of her actions instead took the form of speeches and the written word.

The threat of violence and terrorism from anarchist groups was a great fear in the late 19th and early 20th century. An anarchist, Leon Czolgosz, assassinated President William McKinley in 1901 and an anarchist group bombed a building in lower Manhattan in 1920. But there were dozens more episodes. Violence in the name of freedom was consistent with the ideas of most anarchists and Goldman as well. She believed, however, that anarchism was an ideology that could stop the violence perpetrated on working people by those who held power, wealth and influence. The following quote from Goldman sums up her very idealistic understanding of her political philosophy:

> Anarchism, then, really stands for the liberation of the human mind from the dominion of religion; the liberation of the human body from the dominion of property; liberation from the shackles and restraint of government. Anarchism stands for a social order based on the free grouping of individuals for the purpose of producing real social wealth; an order that will guarantee to every human being free access to the earth and full enjoyment of the necessities of life, according to individual desires, tastes, and inclinations.[3]

For Goldman anarchism could bring real freedom. Religion, she believed, denied humans rational thought that could expand human knowledge. Capitalism, according to Goldman, pursued only profit for investors and not profit for the community, and government used both religion and capitalism to keep the masses in subjugation to the wealthy and powerful. By doing away with religion, capitalism and government Goldman believed that humans would initiate a society of mutual support, which would lead to real freedom, self-definition and self-determination, for all people regardless of race, gender or sexual preference.

Significantly, Goldman extended her philosophy to the lives of women. During most of her life women had very few rights. Women could not vote prior to 1920, they were restricted in marriage to male subordination, and their sexual function and preference was not entirely theirs to control. Goldman advocated birth control for women as a means to take control of their lives, and not merely live in the role of human breeders. She also supported "free-love" where consenting adults could be free to couple with those they desired without the restrictions of marriage or the conventions that prohibited homosexuality. Goldman proposed a radical feminism, which attempted to secure more than the right to vote that many of her contemporary woman's rights activists sought. For that reason Goldman was ahead of her time in demanding reproductive rights and birth control, as well as calling for protections for homosexual relationships, or sex outside of marriage. The pursuit of happiness meant just that—if it makes you happy and harms no one else, how should the community or government impede your actions. Goldman believed that American society needed to be remade in order for real freedom to be realized, and for that purpose in 1909 she wrote a new version of America's founding document.

"A New Declaration of Independence," by Emma Goldman is the second famous re-writing of the original declaration drafted for the Continental Congress amidst the American Revolution. The first re-writing came in 1848 by another woman's rights activist, Elizabeth Cady Stanton. While Stanton was critical of an American political system that denied women the right to vote, did not give women full property rights, and gave women less access to education and social prestige, she did have faith that the system in the United States was capable of incorporating women into its design of freedom. Goldman did not agree. As can be seen in her declaration, the United States was a construct that denied freedom, and that was especially true for women. In the beginning of the essay, Goldman indicts government as the main obstacle to human freedom. In the original version penned by Jefferson and the other male "Founding Fathers," these men held it to be true that men erected government to protect freedom, but in practice that freedom was only for the benefit of educated, wealthy, white men—at least at that time. The truth that Goldman held as self-evident was that government protected inequality by favoring those who controlled the economic and political systems. In her writing the government and those who control it are clearly referenced as male, but the country itself is significantly denoted as female. The weapons of the male system, war, nationalism, religion, the pursuit of wealth, brought misery and destruction to the people. For Goldman only individuals acting on behalf of their common interests without institutional forms could develop a society of peace and prosperity.

QUESTIONS FOR FURTHER DISCUSSION

- How does Goldman's use of the wording and form of the original Declaration of Independence affect an American reader? What effect do you think she had in mind?

- Goldman uses gender in the document to further her political philosophy. How is this accomplished? Is it effective?

- What is Goldman's problem with group affiliations? How do group associations create a power dynamic of haves and have-nots? Do you think that Goldman believes all group associations are bad, or only those formed in a national and religious context?

- Do you get a sense of Goldman's solution to the evils she describes? Are they really evil? Are there really solutions?

NOTES

1. Kathy E. Fergusen, *Emma Goldman: Political Thinking in the Streets*, 26.
2. Theodore Roosevelt, "Address to Congress" December, 1901.
3. Emma Goldman, *Anarchism and Other Essays* (New York, 1917), 62.

BIBLIOGRAPHY/SUGGESTED READINGS

Avrich, Paul. *Anarchist Voices: An Oral History of Anarchism in America*, 2005.

Chalberg, John. *Emma Goldman: American Individualist*, 2008.

Ehrlich, Howard J. ed. *Reinventing Anarchy, Again*, 1978.

Fergusen, Kathy. *Emma Goldman: Political Thinking in the Streets*, 2011.

Haaland, Bonnie. *Emma Goldman: Sexuality and the Impurity of the State*, 1993.

Marsh, Margaret. *Anarchist Women, 1870–1920*, 1981.

Fascist Ideology:
The Italian Case Study

Jeffrey LaMonica

The right to national independence does not arise from any merely literary and idealistic form of self-consciousness; still less from a more or less passive and unconscious *de facto* situation, but from an active, self-conscious, political will expressing itself in action and ready to prove its rights. It arises, in short, from the existence, at least *in fieri*, of a State. Indeed, it is the State which, as the expression of a universal ethical will, creates the right to national independence. . . . As for the individual, so for the nation, and so for mankind. Hence the high value of culture in all its forms (artistic, religious, scientific) and the outstanding importance of education. Hence also the essential value of work, by which man subjugates nature and creates the human world (economic, political, ethical, and intellectual).

—Benito Mussolini and Giovanni Gentile, *The Doctrine of Fascism*, 1935

INTRODUCTION

An analyses of Benito Mussolini and Giovanni Gentile's 1932 article "The Doctrine of Fascism" reveals nationalism, imperialism, militarism, pragmatism, and authoritarian liberalism as the primary tenets of Italian fascism. Fascism is typically associated with sweeping nefarious terms such as "dictatorship," "oppression," "war," and "genocide." This stigma is largely the result of the vilification of fascism after the horrors of the Second World War. Nevertheless, "The Doctrine of Fascism" articulates Italian fascist ideology as far more than just arbitrary autocracy, tyranny, and violence. Like all ideologies, however, fascism is subject to the test of "theory versus reality." Identifying the core ideological principles pronounced in "The Doctrine of Fascism" and measuring the extent to which Italy actualized these tenets are the goals of this study.

The Fascist Italian Government published Mussolini and Gentile's "The Doctrine of Fascism" three years after it was written to refute international perceptions of fascism as a capricious ideology devoid of an actual creed. Beneath its radical and extreme veneer, Italian fascism was not unlike other political ideologies in terms of its formation and structure. It borrowed from a multitude of existing philosophies in the 1920s and 1930s as it attempted to interpret the past, analyze the present, and aspire to the future. For example, the Italian artist and writer F. T. Marinetti had employed the rhetoric of nationalism, imperialism,

Fascist Italian Postage Stamp Depicting Hitler and Mussolini

militarism, pragmatism, and authoritarian liberalism a decade prior to the emergence of Italian fascism in his 1909 "The Founding and Manifesto of Futurism."

NATIONALISM

Nationalism was the fundamental principle of Italian fascist ideology and the basis for all other components of Italian fascism. Italian fascism's concept of the state as the embodiment of all citizens and the government and military as the instruments of popular will represented the extreme civic nationalism at the heart of every political decision in Fascist Italy. The state and the people were one, therefore, the government made decisions based on an assumed popular consent. Hannah Ardent's *The Origins of Totalitarianism* describes this self-determination based on civic nationalism as Fascist Italy's attempt to provide an alternative to the classic liberal concept of the people, the government, and the military as separate entities.[1] Needless to say, civic nationalism as the basis of popular consent for government decisions and military action differs drastically from the classic liberal notion of consensus through electoral processes. For example, when Fascist Italy's army invaded Ethiopia in 1935, Mussolini announced publically that "It is not only an army marching towards its goal, but it is forty-four million Italians marching in unity behind this army."[2] Mussolini did not intend this to be a figurative statement.

Ethnic nationalism can be seen in Italian fascism's endorsement of the biological supremacy of those living within the state and xenophobia toward those outside of it. The ethnic connection between the Italian people and their fascist leaders further solidified the links between government decisions, military action, and popular will. The war with Ethiopia spawned the formation of Fascist Italy's Ministry of Popular Culture. The ministry published propaganda postcards and posters, produced films and radio programs, and monitored school curricula.[3] Classic liberal societies deem this level of government manipulation of information as scandalous. In an Italian fascist society bound by civic and ethnic nationalism, however, the public embraced the government's interpretation of the truth as their own. Propaganda proved to be an effective tool for defining Italian ethnic identity by contrasting it with foreigners, such as Italy's Ethiopian enemy. For example, postcards created by Aurelio Bertiglia for the Ministry of Popular Culture in 1935 portray cartoons of Italian children in dapper military uniforms dutifully distributing food to hungry Ethiopian children wrapped in traditional robes. The Italian children appear distinctly more mature than the Ethiopian children who are kneeling on the ground with their eager eyes wide open and fingers in their mouths.

IMPERIALISM

Imperialism, justified by both civic and ethnic nationalism, was another core tenet of Italian fascism. Mussolini and Gentile's article showcased Fascist Italy's imperialist ideology, "the state . . . is also power . . . felt and respected beyond its own frontiers. This implies . . . expansion." It also ties imperialism to nationalism, "An imperial nation . . . is a leader of others . . . the imperialistic spirit . . . a manifestation of their vitality."[4] The invasion of Ethiopia provided the Fascist Government with a nationalist imperialist centerpiece for rallying the Italian people. In a 1935 statement to the *London Times* regarding the attack on Ethiopia, Benito Mussolini made Social Darwinist claims about Fascist Italy bringing "modern civilization" to Africa. Furthermore, Mussolini announced to the League of Nations that the Italian Army was not invading Ethiopia, but carrying out a

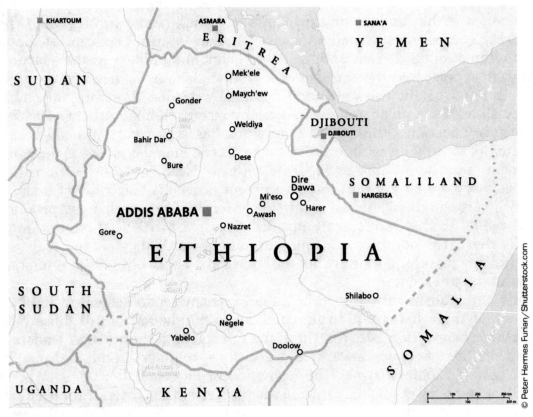

Map of Ethiopia

"civilizing mission." Renato Micheli's famous 1935 propaganda poem *Little Black Face* describes a young Ethiopian girl as "a slave among slaves" and an Italian soldier as her liberator. In an instance of life imitating art, the Viceroy and Governor-General of Italian East Africa Prince Amedeo of Aosta abolished feudalism in Ethiopia in 1937 and redistributed land to nearly a half a million former serfs.[5]

MILITARISM

Militarism, fueled by nationalism and as a means to imperialism, was also a basic pillar of Italian fascism. The military, like the Italian people, was inseparable from the Fascist Government. Benito Mussolini used militarization to unify and mobilize the populous by encouraging the formation of paramilitary social, athletic, and student organizations across Italy in the 1930s. This initiative targeted the youth in particular, for they represented the future of Fascist Italy.[6] For example, *The Pebble Hisses*, a popular anthem of the Italian Fascist Youth or *Balilla*, reflects fascist nationalist attitudes toward conformity and nonconformity. The hymn proclaims that the *Balilla* will give their hearts to those who stand with them and throw stones at those who oppose them.

"The Doctrine of Fascism" rejects peace as an unrealistic aspiration running counter to both human nature and international order, "Fascism does not . . . believe in the possibility or utility of perpetual peace." In 1909, "The Founding and Manifesto of Futurism" predicted an Italy where, "Except in struggle, there is no more beauty" and "We will glorify war—the world's only hygiene-militarism, patriotism. . . ."[7] Fascist Italy held its military capabilities and successes as the primary variables for measuring its national worth. Italy's army, navy, and military victories provided tangible reinforcement for the civic and ethnic nationalism of the Italian people in the 1930s.

PRAGMATISM

Pragmatic leadership, where ends always justified means, was another core Italian fascist concept. Italy's parliamentary system ceased to exist by 1925, and even the Grand Council of Fascism was little more than a rubber stamp for Benito Mussolini's decrees. Mussolini and Gentile criticized democratic systems of government for concerning themselves too much with increasing the number of people involved in the decision-making process at the expense of quality choices and decisive action, "Fascism denies that numbers . . . can be the determining factor" in government policies.[8] Plebiscites and bureaucratic checks and balances were seen as unnecessary obstructions to government decision-making in Fascist Italy. The Italian Fascist Government only needed civic and ethnic nationalism as its mandate from the people. Dispensing with standard procedures and constitutionalism allowed the Fascist Government to develop policies aimed at immediate objectives by any methods necessary.

Pragmatism allowed Mussolini's government to ally itself with non-fascist seats of power in Italian society, such as the Roman Catholic Church, the Italian Nationalist Association, big business, and labor unions, to achieve national goals. Arendt's *The Origins of Totalitarianism* refers to this unencumbered decision-making as "actualism" and considers it to be one of the strengths of Italian fascism.[9] "The Doctrine of Fascism" asserts that, "In politics, fascism aims at realism." Fascist nationalism bound the people, the government, and the military together in a concerted pursuit of objectives superseding lofty ideals and democratic processes. Mussolini and Gentile stated that fascism was an "educator" and "law-giver," whose "doctrine must . . . be a vital act and not a verbal display." Marinetti's 1909 publication had rejected idealism as "pensive immobility" and proclaimed that Italians "intend to exalt aggressive action."[10]

AUTHORITARIAN LIBERALISM

Finally, Italian fascism was grounded in the precept of authoritarian liberalism, a seemingly oxymoronic concept through the lens of classic liberalism. It posited that it was not necessary for a society to have a democratic system of government to realize liberal rights and freedoms for its people. Authoritarian liberalism stemmed from Italian fascism's nationalist assertion that the people, the government, and the military were symbiotic. Mussolini and Gentile referred to "the nation and . . . individuals . . . bound together by a moral law . . . founded on duty" and "the renunciation of self-interest." Fascist Italy sought to attain a liberal society through nationalist consent instead of democratic consensus. Mussolini and Gentile claimed that the fascist "state" was "based on broad foundations of popular support" with "millions of individuals who . . . are ready to serve."[11] Elie Kedourie's *Nationalism* compares multiple forms of government and asserts that decisions reached through democratic processes are just as arbitrary and guided by misinformation as ones attained through authoritarian decree.[12] The history of slavery and racial segregation in the United States is evidence that democratic systems of government are not synonymous with freedom and rights.

The fascist government in Italy believed in providing an orderly environment in which individuals and institutions enjoyed the right and freedom to reach their potential. "The Doctrine of Fascism" claims that, "no human or spiritual values can exist" outside of the state. It asserts that "man . . . as an individual" is "self-centered, subject to natural law, which instinctively urges him toward a life of selfish momentary pleasure." In Italian fascist society, "The state educates the citizens . . . of their mission" and "harmonizes their divergent interests." Arendt's *The Origins of Totalitarianism* contends that individual rights and freedoms cannot be realized without a government, democratic or otherwise, to implement and enforce them.[13] For example, Fascist Italy's Vidoni Pact and Rocco Law exemplified authoritarian liberal legislation. Both laws converted Italy into a corporate capitalist economy in the mid-1920s by establishing the Fascist Government as the permanent arbiter between big business and labor unions. In this capacity, the government was responsible for maintaining fair businesses practices and protecting the rights of Italian workers.[14]

Italian fascism envisioned itself as a liberal revolutionary political phenomena, not a conservative reactionary movement. It did not seek to reverse the established principles of classic liberalism and reassert the Old Regime in Italy. Instead, Italian fascism pursued many of the same goals as classic liberalism, but rejected liberalism's insistence upon democratic methodology. "The Doctrine of Fascism" refers to this flaw in classic liberalism as the "lie of political equalitarianism." In "Democratic regimes . . . people are . . . deluded into the belief that they exercise sovereignty, while all the time real sovereignty resides in . . . secret forces."[15] In this regard, Italian fascism represented a more honest form of government decision-making than representative democracy.

CONCLUSION

From the perspectives of classic liberal societies in the 1920s and 1930s, Fascist Italy was a nation without a democratic system of government and, therefore, devoid of rights and freedoms. American journalist John Bond referred to Italy as a despotic dictatorship that rejected democracy for the sake of silencing political opposition in his 1929 book *Mussolini: The Wild Man of Europe.* Bond's book also portrays Benito Mussolini's pragmatism as self-serving, "The changes in Mussolini's political and social creed . . . have always been accompanied by an advance in his personal fortunes."[16] These kinds of sweeping negative commentaries blinded much of the outside world to the actual ideology of Italian Fascism.

Remaining true to the ideological principle of authoritarian liberalism while pursuing national interests domestically and abroad proved untenable for the Italian Fascist Government. This balancing act usually resulted in dictatorial measures limiting the rights and freedoms of the Italian people. This dilemma is in no way unique to Fascist Italy. Most governments and political parties around the world compromise their ideological aspirations to confront the real challenges of leadership; but through the negative lenses of foreign journalists from classic liberal cultures, Fascist Italy appeared tyrannical and oppressive to the outside world. This international facade, while not wholly inaccurate, represented a gross oversimplification of Italian fascist ideology.

To expedite its plan to industrialize Italy according to a corporate capitalist model, the Fascist Government's role as mediator between big business and labor unions became increasingly bureaucratic, unwieldy, and ultimately corrupt by the 1930s. Benito Mussolini's attempts to reverse Italy's population decline included encroachments on civil liberties, such as quotas for women in the workplace, taxes on adult males who remained single, and anti-homosexuality legislation.[17] Furthermore, security concerns pushed fascist policies toward heavy handed measures. After three assassination attempts by political terrorists, Mussolini abolished local elections, banned non-fascist political parties, and formed the Organization for Vigilance and Repression of Anti-Fascism (OVRA) to investigate and prosecute political dissidents. OVRA monitored, harassed, and incarcerated many prominent Italian intellectuals, such as Primo Levi and Antonio Gramsci.[18]

Establishing a civic and ethnic nationalist identity in a country with a long tradition of extreme sectional differences presented an additional challenge for the Fascist Government. Ethnic Slavs in northeastern Italy continually resisted assimilation and became a regular target of OVRA persecution. Additionally, fascist nationalism never overrode the economic and cultural differences between Italy's urban industrial north and rural agricultural south. Local fascist leaders in southern Italy and Sicily set aside nationalism to govern over the agrarian peasantry of these provincial regions.[19]

Even Fascist Italy's militarist and imperialist aspirations produced unexpected side effects and often fell short of expectations. In 1929, John Bond reported that the Fascist Government's robust military spending was draining funds from Italy's social welfare programs. Drastic cultural and linguistic differences blocked the Fascist Government from transplanting its ideology in Ethiopia. In fact, Benito Mussolini never even visited the colony after his army subdued it in 1937.[20] The most tangible aspect of Italian Fascism in east Africa was a giant bust of Mussolini in the desert outside the town of Adowa. American news correspondent Boake Carter's 1935 book *Black Shirt, Black*

Skin claims that Mussolini spoke of the invasion of Ethiopia as the glorious beginning of a new fascist Roman Empire when, in reality, it was about pillaging Africa's natural resources.[21] Bond's book discusses how Mussolini's militarism, particularly Italian naval expansion in the Mediterranean Sea, was causing Fascist Italy to fall out of favor with Great Britain, France, and the League of Nations.[22] This sort of military posturing would eventually lead to Fascist Italy's undoing during the Second World War.

Arendt's *The Origins of Totalitarianism* argues that Fascist Italy was never fully totalitarian, because the Fascist Government never considered itself superior to the other segments of Italian society. According to Arendt, the government, the military, big business, labor unions, and the people were equal components of an Italian fascist society bound by nationalism. Arendt also cites Fascist Italy's high tolerance for ideological opposition as another one of its non-totalitarian traits, especially in comparison to Nazi Germany. Prior to the Second World War, the Fascist Government seldom employed its death penalty against political dissidents. Instead, Mussolini usually sent his opponents into exile and confinement on penal islands in the Tyrrhenian Sea.[23]

Ultimately, Benito Mussolini's obsession with realizing the ideological tenets of imperialism and militarism led to the demise of Italian fascism in 1945. By the end of the Second World War, Mussolini was dead, Italian fascism was no more, and Italy was in shambles. Italy's tryst with fascism may have been more a result of the Italian people's utilitarian approach to politics than the opportunism of Mussolini and his Blackshirts. After all, it was popular support that enabled the Fascist Party to assume power in Italy in 1922 and the complete loss of that popular support which resulted in Mussolini's execution in 1945. Furthermore, unlike Germany, Italy did not go through the painful process of denazification after the war.[24] Not only have modern-day Italians purged fascism from their popular memory and cultural heritage, but fascism is illegal in Italy today. The Fascist Party's attempt to transform traditional regionalism into civic and ethnic nationalism failed as well. Regional Italian cultural identities remain very strong in the early twentieth century. Italy's North League or *Lega Nord* continues to advocate for the cultural and political separation of northern and southern Italy.

QUESTIONS FOR FURTHER DISCUSSION

- In which ways did Fascist Italy succeed and/or fail to realize the ideological principles of fascism?

- Is it possible for a government to follow fascist ideology and, at the same time, allow its people to enjoy liberal rights and freedoms?

- Considering the ideological tenets described in Benito Mussolini and Giovanni Gentile's 1932 article "The Doctrine of Fascism," is it inevitable that fascism will always lead to war and/or genocide?

NOTES

1. Hannah Arendt, *The Origins of Totalitarianism* (New York: Harcourt, Brace, and World, 1966), 258.

2. Benito Mussolini, "Speech Broadcast, 2 October 1935," http://www.historycentral.com/HistoricalDocuments/Mussolini'sSpeech.html.

3. Alan Cassels, *Fascist Italy* (Wheeling, IL: Harlan Davidson Inc., 1968), 67.

4. Benito Mussolini and Giovanni Gentile, "The Doctrine of Fascism," https://www.google.com/url?sa=t&rct=j&q=&esrc=s&source=web&cd=6&cad=rja&uact=8&ved=0ahUKEw-jmgNWjsvDKAhWFFj4KHVZjDjUQFghCMAU&url=http%3A%2F%2Ffaculty.smu.edu%2Fbkcarter%2FTHE%2520DOCTRINE%2520OF%2520FASCISM.doc&usg=AFQjC-NEYwK_TPGvhuiM_2U3tkkuqEaqb2Q.

5. Benito Mussolini, "Speech to the League of Nations, 21 September 1935," https://teachwar.wordpress.com/resources/war-justifications-archive/italian-ethiopian-abyssinian-war-1935/; Anthony Mockler, *Haile Selassie's War* (New York: Olive Branch Press, 2003), 187.

6. Cassels, 66.

7. Mussolini and Gentile; RJB Bosworth, *Mussolini* (London: Arnold, 2002), 190; FT Marinetti, "The Founding and Manifesto of Futurism," http://www.italianfuturism.org/manifestos/foundingmanifesto/.

8. Mussolini and Gentile.

9. Cassels, 55; Arendt, 325.

10. Mussolini and Gentile; Marinetti.

11. Mussolini and Gentile.

12. Elie Kedourie, *Nationalism* (Cambridge, MA: Blackwell, 1993), 121.

13. Mussolini and Gentile; Hannah Arendt, "The Perplexities of the Rights of Man," in *The Portable Hannah Arendt*, edited by Peter Baehr (New York: Penguin Books, 2000), 32, 43.

14. Cassels, 57, 62.

15. Mussolini and Gentile.

16. John Bond, *Mussolini: The Wild Man of Europe* (Washington, DC: Independent Publishing Co., 1929), 64, 111, 197.

17. Cassels, 57, 68; Bosworth, 231.

18. Bosworth, 219, 231; Cassels, 69.

19. Bosworth, 222, 228, 292.

20. Mockler, 154, 186.

21. Bond, 198; Boake Carter, *Black Shirt, Black Skin* (Harrisburg, PA: Telegraph Press, 1935), 119, 95.

22. Bond, 84; Carter, 121.

23. Arendt, *The Origins of Totalitarianism*, 257, 259, 308.

24. Cassels, 75.

BIBLIOGRAPHY/SUGGESTED READINGS

Books

Arendt, Hannah. "The Perplexities of the Rights of Man." In *The Portable Hannah Arendt*, edited by Peter Baehr 31–45. New York: Penguin Books, 2000.

Arendt, Hannah. *The Origins of Totalitarianism*. New York: Harcourt, Brace, and World, 1966.

Bond, John. *Mussolini: The Wild Man of Europe*. Washington, DC: Independent Publishing Co., 1929.

Bosworth, RJB. *Mussolini*. New York: Oxford University Press, 2002.

Carter, Boake. *Black Shirt, Black Skin*. Harrisburg, PA: Telegraph Press, 1935.

Cassels, Alan. *Fascist Italy*. Wheeling, IL: Harlan Davidson Inc., 1968.

Kedourie, Elie. *Nationalism*. Cambridge, MA: Blackwell, 1993.

Mockler, Anthony. *Haile Selassie's War*. New York: Olive Branch Press, 2003.

Online Documents

Marinetti, FT. "The Founding and Manifesto of Futurism." 1909. Accessed April 1, 2016. http://www.italianfuturism.org/manifestos/foundingmanifesto/

Mussolini, Benito and Giovanni Gentile. "The Doctrine of Fascism." 1932. Accessed February 11, 2016. https://www.google.com/url?sa=t&rct=j&q=&esrc=s&source=web&cd=6&cad=rja&uact=8&ved=0ahUKEwjmgNWjsvDKAhWFFj4KHVZjDjUQFghCMAU&url=http%3A%2F%2Ffaculty.smu.edu%2Fbkcarter%2FTHE%2520DOCTRINE%2520OF%2520FASCISM.doc&usg=AFQjCNEYwK_TPGvhuiM_2U3tkkuqEaqb2Q

Mussolini, Benito. "Speech Broadcast, 2 October 1935." 1935. Accessed April 19, 2016. http://www.historycentral.com/HistoricalDocuments/Mussolini'sSpeech.html

Mussolini, Benito. "Speech to the League of Nations, 21 September 1935." 1935. Accessed April 19, 2016. https://teachwar.wordpress.com/resources/war-justifications-archive/italian-ethiopian-abyssinian-war-1935/

CHAPTER II

Ideology and Culture

Cold War Counter-Culture: Dissent West and East

Matthew Kowalski

A comfortable, smooth, reasonable, democratic un-freedom prevails in advanced industrial civilization, a token of technical progress. Indeed, what could be more rational than the suppression of individuality in the mechanization of socially necessary but painful performances; the concentration of individual enterprises in more effective, more productive corporations; the regulation of free competition among unequally equipped economic subjects; the curtailment of prerogatives and national sovereignties which impede the international organization of resources. That this technological order also involves a political and intellectual coordination may be a regrettable and yet promising development.

—Herbert Marcuse, *One Dimensional Man*, 1964

The profound difference between our system—in terms of the nature of power—and what we traditionally understand by dictatorship, a difference I hope is clear even from this quite superficial comparison, has caused me to search for some term appropriate for our system, purely for the purposes of this essay. If I refer to it henceforth as a 'post-totalitarian' system, I am fully aware that this is perhaps not the most precise term, but I am unable to think of a better one. I do not wish to imply by the prefix 'post' that the system is no longer totalitarian; on the contrary, I mean that it is totalitarian in a way fundamentally different from classical dictatorships, different from totalitarianism as we usually understand it.

—Vaclav Havel, *The Power of the Powerless*, 1979

INTRODUCTION

In late 1968, the US Central Intelligence Agency reported that 'counter-cultural activists' were both active and disruptive in every corner of the globe. The report, entitled "Restless Youth," characterized the era's mass protests movements as a truly "worldwide phenomenon."[1] That year had already witnessed massive student protests in the United States, West Germany, Spain, Japan, and South Korea. Similar protests in both France and Italy saw student demonstrators joined by young workers, which only added to the unease of traditional ruling elites. Dissent was also causing conflict within the so-called 'Socialist Bloc' (particularly in Czechoslovakia, Poland, and Yugoslavia) and in various 'Third World' nations, such as Chile and Tunisia.[2]

The profoundly globalized nature of the student protests of the late sixties raises an important question for scholars. How and more importantly why did young people separated by opposing sides of the Cold War ideological divide find themselves participating in practically the same kind of protest movements? Indeed, the core concerns of counter-cultural activists on both sides of the Cold War divide were remarkably similar. These youthful dissenters openly rebelled against the post-World War II cultural consensus of their parents. They challenged the alienation, limits on creative individuality, and a lack of 'authenticity'[3] that they felt characterized their increasingly technocratic-consumerist driven cultures. This critique of social conformity was expressed in a shared trans-national language of rock music, beat poetry, and abstract forms of artistic expression.[4] Counter-cultural activists in both the capitalist 'West' and the socialist 'East' also shared a similar social composition. Unlike the protest movements for the early twentieth century or Third World revolutionaries, these were not the socially-economically downtrodden. Rather, they represented the privileged children of highly industrial societies that had achieved historically unprecedented standards of living. Although the space allowed for and the stakes attached to engaging in dissent were sometimes radically different, the rise of a truly global counter-culture forces us to call into question many of the essential assumptions about the nature of the 'East-West' divide.[5]

COUNTER-CULTURE: A COLD WAR CREATION?

Despite their antagonistic ideologies and visions for the future, both the capitalist and socialist blocs engaged in remarkably similar post-war reconstruction programs. The sacrifices of ordinary citizens during the Second World War contributed to an almost universal sentiment for radical social-economic change. For the liberal democracies, the old pre-war models of *laissez-faire* capitalism had proved inadequate in the face of both the Great Depression and the ideological challenges from radical anti-liberal forces. Post-war democracy had to be reinvented to include a welfare component that would protect not only civil but also social-economic rights. As one commentator put it, "if we speak of democracy, we do not mean a democracy which maintains the right to vote but forgers the right to work and the right to live."[6] Following this premise, both the United States and western European nations pumped massive resources into post-war social programs. These included programs that would open up opportunities for affordable housing, health care, and higher education. Unemployment, which was seen as a key contributor in the rise of inter-war fascism, was augmented by a strong public sector economy.[7] In addition to this, the increased purchasing power of ordinary citizens contributed to the rise of expansive consumer culture.

This need for reform also found fertile ground in the emerging Socialist Bloc in Central and Eastern Europe. Despite the fact that these regimes were very real police states, public opinion was still an impor-tant factor in policy making. The late Stalinist period did see some attempts by the Soviet state to meet the rising expectations of its citizens.[8] Limited moves were made to shift Soviet economic planning away from heavy industry to the production of consumer goods. After Stalin's death in 1953 and the onset of the Khrushchev 'Thaw', these reforms were intensified. The post-Stalin Soviet leadership placed an emphasis on providing Soviet citizens with better communal housing. Much like suburbanization in the United States, the new *Khruschyovka* apartments became a symbol for post-war prosperity.[9] Simultaneously, Eastern Bloc regimes placed a premium on the development of light industry and the creation of a form of 'socialist consumerism.' With the reduction of large-scale state terror and other coercive measures after the mid-fifties, the socialist regimes used the 'soft-power' of plentiful consumer goods to win over the loyalty of the populations which they governed. Fear of arrest and ideological purity were slowly replaced by visions of a 'socialist good life.' This would include private housing, a television, a car, and a kitchen stuffed with the latest in mass-produced consumer commodities. All of this, while still reaping the benefits of the expansive Soviet-style welfare state that guaranteed its populations 'cradle to grave' employment, health care, and higher education.

A Soviet Grocery Store in the 1970s

The development of post-war consumer societies in both the capitalist and socialist worlds, however, was also conditioned by the development of the global Cold War. This 'good life', be it capitalist suburbia or the new socialist kitchen, was part and parcel of the larger Cold War project of 'winning hearts and minds.' The Cold War was at its core as much a cultural struggle as it was a diplomatic-political event.[10] As such, each side of the conflict used their post-war economic successes as a tool in a larger global contest for hegemony. Consumption and rising standards of living were never divorced from ideology.[11] Indeed, the premium that both sides in the Cold War placed on state-funded higher education and the promotion of various 'specialists' was always explicitly tied to international objectives. Film, music, and sport were also enlisted into the Cold War arsenals of both camps. Success in 'marketing' your ideology was seen as the best way to secure loyalty both at home and in the international arena.[12]

The main beneficiaries of this cultural Cold War was the trans-national 'baby-boom'[13] generation. It was youth that reaped the main benefits of post-war modernization, with access to opportunities their parents' generation could not have dreamed of. However, Cold War elites shared concerns about the moral and ideological fiber of this new generation. Policy makers feared a malaise and the erosion of traditional values. As early as 1960, West German chancellor Konrad Adenhauer lamented the fact that, "the most important problem of our day is the 'inner' political weakness and superficiality of daily life."[14] Soviet politicians were equally concerned by what they perceived to be a growing public disillusionment with the 'Communist Project' and an autonomous youth culture that seemed to lack the ideological fervor of their parents who had both constructed 'Socialism' and defeated fascism in the previous decades. The answer for Cold War elites was to deliberately encourage the mass mobilization of youth in the service of the Cold War.[15] Elites explicitly politicized their young people, telling them that the future rested in their hands. As we shall see, this polarization would have unforeseen consequences.

RAGING AGAINST THE MACHINE IN THE CAPITALIST WEST

The work of the German émigré philosopher, Herbert Marcuse, probably best exemplifies the unintended consequences of Cold War prosperity in the capitalist 'First World.' Influenced by both the Frankfurt School's neo-Marxist critique of industrial modernity, the 'creative force' of non-western guerrilla fighters, and the Chinese Cultural Revolution,[16] Marcuse attacked some of the basic premises of post-war progress. For Marcuse, modern industrial society and consumerism repressed individuality in a sea of increasing standardization. Far from liberating mankind, industrialization had in fact served to prevent free and 'natural' fulfillment. Indeed, he went as far as to suggest that highly technocratic societies actually 'denaturalized' humanity from their basic instincts.[17] Modern civilization, for Marcuse, was a 'disciplinary civilization' that enforced mass conformity and stifled growth. A civilization that was fundamentally shallow and alienating.

This critique of conformity was closely tied to the larger Cold War project. For Marcuse, Cold War thinking was 'one dimensional thought'[18] that was incapable of moving beyond basic binaries. Everything was boiled down to simply 'good vs. evil,' 'black vs. white,' 'free vs. slave' or 'capitalist vs. communist.' In essence, Marcuse characterized the Cold War contest and the social-economic-cultural structures that it produced as being inherently totalitarian.[19] In addition to his full-frontal assault on the logic of Cold War binaries, Marcuse was one of the earliest counter-culture voices to stress the similarities between the capitalist and socialist versions of industrial modernity. For Marcuse, the inherently totalitarian logic of Western industrial society had its twin counterpart in the Eastern Bloc.[20]

Marcuse's twin critique of post-war industrialism and the Cold War found a ready audience in the young student radicals of the sixties. Well educated and full of expectations for the future, the global counter-culture found a voice to express their increasing reservations about the potential of the societies in which they lived. Global events, such as the war in Vietnam, seemed to expose the contradictions imbedded in Cold War logic. As these young men and women were taught to think 'ideologically,' activism and dissent were natural reactions. The very mechanism that underwrote post-war pros-perity helped create a counter-culture that would serve to challenge it. A generation of increasingly mobile and disenchanted young people demanded more out of their par-ents' societies. Material abundance was for them not a substitute for cultural or individ-ual pursuits. In fact, many viewed the universe of the 'suburban good life' as downright imprisoning. As feminist icon Betty Friedan put it, "a cozy concentration camp."[21]

POST-TOTALITARIANISM AND THE STRUGGLE AGAINST CONFORMITY IN THE EAST

While the nature of the socialist societies in the Eastern Bloc prevented the kind of open dissent witnessed in the capitalist 'West,' elites were faced with similar challenges. Despite massive material advantages, youth in Central and Eastern Europe also increas-ingly felt alienated from existing power structures. For many, the promises of the initial wave of the post-Stalinist reforms seemed increasingly limited. Hopes that state social-ism could reform itself along more humanist lines were brutally crushed in Hungary in 1956 and Czechoslovakia in 1968. Public signs of unconformity, especially western cultural imports such as rock and roll,[22] were not tolerated. Socialist youth increasingly began to 'check-out' of the public sphere and engage in private life.[23]

This retreat into the private sphere was partially fostered by the social-economic-cultural realities of what would be called 'Late Socialism.' Following both the removal of Khrushchev in 1964 and the crushing of the reform minded regime in Czechoslovakia in 1968, authorities hit upon a clever means of stratifying the population's ever increas-ing material demands while simultaneously keeping a lid on dissent.[24] Realizing that return to Stalinist mass arrests was impossible, Socialist regimes offered their popula-tions a new 'socialist social contract' in the sixties. Ordinary citizens would be offered the material benefits (work, consumer goods, etc.) in exchange for public displays of loyalty. This transformation was buttressed by a deliberate de-emphasis on ideology and forms of mass participation. As long as citizens conformed to social norms and engaged in public rituals,[25] such as attending Communist Party meetings, celebrating official holidays, and voting in totally meaningless Soviet-style elections, the state would essentially let them retreat into their private sphere.

It was this culture of unauthenticity that dissents, such as Czech playwright Vaclav Havel, had to contend with. Much like their counter-cultural contemporaries in the capitalist world, the heart of their critique was aimed at rescuing the individual in a modern society that enforced conformity. In both cases, the means that power struc-tures used to enforce this conformity was not so much naked coercion or mass ter-ror, but rather through the mechanisms of cultural 'soft power' and the practices of modern consumerism.[26] This is the crucial distinction Havel makes between classical totalitarianism and what he refers to as post-totalitarianism. For him, as indeed for the counter-cultural activists on the other side of the Cold War ideological divide, the only solution to the alienating pressures of the system was to engage in 'people power.' Although the risks attached to dissent were certainly much higher for Havel and other Central and Eastern Europeans, the roots of their resistance to authority were firmly planted in the trans-national consumer cultures that emerged in both the capitalist and socialist camps following the Second World War.

CONCLUSION

In a fairly recent interview, German chancellor and former East German citizen Angela Merkel reflected on the similarities and differences between the sixties counter-culture in the 'West' vs. the 'East.' According to Merkel: "One side wanted to break-up socialism and make it more humane, but had no aversions to the social market. The other side had a free market economy background and glorified socialism. Basically, these were opposing movements, and yet in some ways they are the same."[27] While she is correct in pointing out some of the critical differences between youth movements on opposing sides of the East-West divide, her comments still underline the prevalence of Marcuse's 'one dimensional thinking' when it comes to thinking about the Cold War. When one closely examines both the causes and the content of the dissent movements of the global sixties, however, this binary view of the Cold War is certainly ripe of reinterpretation. Rather than creating our own 'intellectual borders,' we should begin to strive to look at the Cold War as a truly trans-national event. Only then can it fully be integrated into a legitimate global narrative of the twentieth century.

German Chancellor Angela Merkel in 2015

QUESTIONS FOR FURTHER DISCUSSION

- Un-pack Marcuse's concept of 'one dimensional' thinking. How, and more importantly why, does he locate the roots of this phenomenon in modern industrial society? Does he see a major difference between Western free-market capitalism and Soviet-style 'state socialism'? Why or why not?

- Describe the system Havel refers to as 'post totalitarianism.' How does this system enforce 'symbolic conformity'? Who ultimately serves as the 'police' in such a system? Would you consider this kind of system 'stable'? Why or why not? Can we make any comparisons between Havel's 'post-totalitarian' society and our own? Explain.

- What roll does consumerism and consumer practice play in both of these texts? Do you think this is an important facet of our author's arguments? If so, why or why not?

NOTES

1. CIA report, "Restless Youth." September 1968, Folder: Youth and Student Movements, Box 13, Files of Walt W. Rostow, National Security File, Lyndon Baines Johnson Library, Austin, Texas.

2. The historian Eric Hobsbawm also reflected upon the "astonishing internationalism of the late sixties student movements" in Eric Hobsbawm, *Age of Extremes: A History of the World, 1914–1991* (New York: Vintage Books, 1994), 326.

3. Jeremi Suri "The Rise and Fall of an International Counterculture, 1960–1975." *AHR*, 114. (September 2009), 46–48.

4. Sergei Zhuk, *Rock and Roll in the Rocket City: The West, Identity, and Ideology in Soviet Dnipropetrovsk, 1960–1985* (Baltimore: John Hopkins University Press 2010), 7–14.

5. There have been a slew of excellent articles and monographs on this very topic published over the last few years. In particular, see Vladimir Tismaneanu's edited volume *Promises of 1968: Crisis, Illusion, and Utopia* (Budapest: Central European University Press, 2011).

6. E. H. Carr from a *Times* opinion piece "The New Europe." See Mark Mazower, *Dark Continent: Europe's Twentieth Century* (New York: Vintage Books, 1998), 185.

7. This was especially acute in West Germany where almost every post-war government viewed favorable unemployment figures as an important facet of their democratic experiment.

8. On this point see Elena Zubkova's excellent *Russia After the War: Hopes, Illusions, and Disappointments, 1945–1957* (London: ME, Shapre, 1998).

9. Susan Reid, "The Khrushchev Kitchen: Domesticating the Scientific-Technological Revolution," *Journal of Contemporary History* 40 (2005), 295.

10. This is increasingly the way scholars of the Cold War are viewing the period. See for example, Tony Shaw and Denise Youngblood's the truly excellent *Cinematic Cold War: The American and Soviet Struggle for Hearts and Minds* (Lawrence: University of Kansas Press, 2010).

11. Yale Richmond, "The 1959 Kitchen Debate (or, how cultural exchanges changed the Soviet Union)," *Russian Life* 52 (2009).

12. See the Introduction to Shaw and Youngblood *Cinematic Cold War.*

13. For an exploration of the Socialist 'Baby Boom' generation see both Vladioslav Zubok's *Zhivago's Children* (Cambridge: Harvard University Press, 2009) and Donald Raleigh's *Soviet Baby Boomers* (London: Oxford University Press, 2001).

14. Suri, "Rise and Fall of an International Counter-Culture." 49.

15. One only needs to consider the various Kennedy era mobilization initiatives, the 'Virgin Lands' campaign of the Khrushchev years, and even the mass-campaigns launched in Maoist China to see this trend cut through Cold War divisions.

16. See Odd Arne Westad's *The Global Cold War: Third World Interventions and the Making of Our Times* (London: Cambridge University Press, 2005).

17. Herbert Marcuse, *Eros and Civilization: A Philosophical Inquiry into Freud* (Boston: Beacon Books, 1955), 197–221.

18. Marcuse, *One Dimensional Man: Studies in the Ideology of Advanced Industrial Society* (Boston, Beacon Books, 1964).

19. See Chapters 10–12 of Hannah Ardent's classic *Origins of Totalitarianism* (New York: Meridian Books, 1958).

20. Chapter One of Marcuse, *One Dimensional Man*.

21. See Betty Friedan, *The Feminine Mystique* (New York: W.W. Norton, 1963).

22. Both Zhuk, *Rock and Roll in the Rocket City* and William Jay Risch's *The Ukrainian West: Culture and the Fate of Empire in Soviet L'viv* (Cambridge: Harvard University Press, 2011).

23. Probably the best work on this subject is Slavenka Drakulic's excellent *How we Survived Communism and Even Laughed* (New York: Harper Perennial, 1993).

24. See Alexei Yurchak, *Everything was Forever, Until it Was No More: The Last Soviet Generation* (Princeton: Princeton University Press, 2006).

25. Paulina Bren, *The Greengrocer and his TV: The Culture of Communism after the1968 Prague Spring* (Ithaca: Cornell University Press, 2010), 7–8.

26. Vaclav Havel, *The Power of the Powerless*.

27. Angela Merkel. From *Suddemdeutsche Zeitlung* (29th February 2009).

BIBLIOGRAPHY/SUGGESTED READINGS

Bren, Paulina. *The Greengrocer and His TV: The Culture of Communism after the 1968 Prague Spring.* Ithaca: Cornell University Press, 2010.

Medovoi, Leerom. *Rebels: Youth and the Cold War Origins of Identity.* Durham, University of North Carolina Press, 2005.

Pontuso, James F. *Vaclav Havel: Civic Responsibility in the Postmodern Age.* New York: Rowman and Littlefield, 2004.

Raleigh, Donald. *Russia's Sputnik Generation: Soviet Baby Boomers Talk About Their Lives.* Bloomington: Indiana University Press, 2006.

Ross, Kristin. *May 68 and Its Afterlives.* Chicago: University of Chicago Press, 2002.

Suri, Jeremi, *Power and Protest: Global Revolution and the Rise of Détente.* Cambridge: Harvard University Press, 2003.

Tismaneanu, Vladimir, ed. *Promises of 1968: Crisis, Illusion, and Utopia.* Budapest Central European University Press, 2011.

"Spoiling the Party": Khrushchev, the Secret Speech, and the Fate of Soviet Socialism

Matthew Kowalski

Far from being a partial retreat, a throwback to the Russian past, or a post-revolutionary betrayal—Stalinism *was* the revolution. It was the 'Stalin Revolution' of the 1930s, not the Bolshevik seizure of power in 1917, that created radically new and durable political, economic, social, and cultural structures that would last for half a century.

—Stephen Kotkin, *Magnetic Mountain*, 1995

INTRODUCTION

When assessing the causes for the dramatic collapse of the Socialist Bloc between the years 1989–1991, historians have offered up a variety of explanations. These have ranged from 'high politics,'[1] to several recent works that have examined these events from a cultural lens.[2] What both of these approaches have stressed is the importance of long-range causes in explaining the decline and the ultimate collapse of the Soviet-style socialist system. Indeed, the story of 1989–1991 would be almost impossible without first referencing the momentous changes that occurred in Socialist society from 1956–1968.[3] Nikita Khrushchev's open (although incomplete) attack on the legacy of former leader Josef Stalin provided the first major challenge to the hegemony of Communist Party of the Soviet Union and the foundations on which Soviet-style socialism was built upon.

STALIN: ARCHITECT OF SOVIET SOCIALISM

Monument to Nikita Khrushchev in Russia

The true importance of Khrushchev's open criticism of Stalin and his legacy needs to be gauged from the larger vantage point of Soviet history. Although the Bolshevik Party under V. I. Lenin had seized state power in 1917, the foundations of what would become Soviet society was only forged during the Stalin revolution of the thirties and the forties. While some commentators and historians have characterized the Stalin era as a retreat or betrayal of the 'pure' Leninist vision,[4] as indeed did Khrushchev himself, it was the massive transformations initiated under Stalin that truly constituted what would become 'Actually Existing Socialism.' The collectivization of agriculture and rapid industrial drives of the First Five Year Plan, transformed what was still a largely peasant based society into a 'modern' urban-industrial nation. While these changes were orchestrated from the top and buttressed by massive state terror, they nevertheless completely altered the fabric of everyday life for Soviet citizens. It was under Stalin that the expansive Soviet welfare state, educational system, and a radically new cultural system were forged. Indeed, it was the Stalin revolution that fundamentally created a unique Soviet form of industrial modernity.[5]

Although Stalin's Soviet Union was unquestionably both propaganda and a police state, this should not be used to dismiss the legitimate popular support the regime enjoyed. As has been pointed out in the scholarly literature on the period, the Stalin-era saw a monumental expansion of social mobility for the average Soviet citizen.[6] This was especially true in the case of women and certain ethno-linguistic minorities. For many, the Stalinist experiment did in fact mean a better standard of living and overall a better life. One must also not forget the massive international capital that the Stalin regime had built up over the course of the thirties and forties. Due to the seemingly impossible achievements of the Soviet modernization drive, leftist movements throughout the globe saw the USSR as the bulwark of progress and liberation.[7] Victory in the Great Patriotic War (World War II) against fascism further cemented the almost mythical status of the Soviet state as the undisputed leader of a worldwide socialist movement. All of the post-war Soviet-style regimes in Central-Eastern Europe[8] and East Asia not only looked to Moscow for inspiration, but largely modelled their socio-economic, political, and cultural systems on the established Stalinist blueprint.

THE THAW YEARS

The main rationale behind Khrushchev's denunciation of Stalinism was an attempt to strengthen the Soviet system. According to Khrushchev, excessive repression and the closed nature of the Stalinist system "were serious obstacles in the path of Soviet social development."[9] For Khrushchev, a return to Leninists principles was necessary to recapture the

Statue of Stalin being Pulled Down in Hungary in 1956

hearts and minds of Soviet citizens. Reform was also seen as a way to help the Soviet state in the global Cold War struggle with the United States. Khrushchev believed that a limited opening up of the Socialist system would encourage both innovation and creativity.[10] As such, a key component of the Khrushchev reforms would be the freer access to information in order to make the Soviet system more competitive.

The new openness in the system took many forms. On the cultural front, Soviet authors and other creative artists could now make limited criticisms of the Stalinist past. Texts such as Aleksandar Solzhenitsyn *One Day in the Life of Ivan Denisovich*, openly dealt with Stalin-era crimes and promoted popular discussions on the legacy of the recent past. Soviet film, which since the early thirties had been forced to conform to the strict aesthetic guidelines of 'Socialist Realism,' could suddenly address a whole series of previously taboo themes.[11] As the fifties went on, Soviet audiences could also start seeing imported films from the outside world. Beginning with the importation of a small number of Indian films, by the end of the decade films from France, Italy, and even a handful from America could be found playing in Soviet theaters.[12]

This newfound cultural openness went hand in hand with the regime's attempt to ease Cold War tensions. Moving away from the Stalinist rhetoric of confrontation, Khrushchev instated a policy of 'Peaceful Coexistence' with the West. Although domestic reforms were always designed to strengthen the Soviet system's competiveness in the Cold War, the Kremlin believed that increased contacts with the outside world could only accelerate the progress of constructing Socialism. Diplomatic openness and trade contacts with the capitalist world would help provide the Soviet state with both hard currency and new technology. Foreign consumer goods would also help buttress the regime's 'hearts and minds' policy by improving the quality of life of ordinary citizens. Indeed, the Khrushchev regime saw material abundance and the creation of a Socialist consumer culture as a critical facet of their attempt to legitimatize the system both at home and abroad.[13] Therefore, contacts with the outside world were deliberately promoted by the state. This was a major departure from the isolationist policies of the Stalin years, when the Soviet regime placed a premium on restricting the free flow of both information and people.

DASHED EXPECTATIONS AND THE UNRAVELING OF THE SOVIET SYSTEM

Although the intentions behind the Khrushchev reforms was to protect and strengthen the Soviet system, the very opposite proved to be the case. Despite its internal flaws, the Stalin system was both stable and insolated the vast majority of the population from potential alternative models of development. The 'Thaw', however, upset this constellation. Because Stalinism was essentially the bedrock of a unique Soviet civilization, open criticism of Stalin quickly led to open questioning of the entire Soviet experiment. Rising standards of living and accesses to foreign goods and ideas also had a corrosive impact. The initial euphoria of the rapid pace of reform created unrealistic expectations amongst the population.[14] Finally, the very limits of state-driven reform were bound to create hostility. Despite the very real opening up of the political system, political dissent was still treated harshly. At the end of the day, the 'Thaw' was always a top-down attempt to strengthen the regime by reforming its more unsavory aspects. It was never conceived as a radical reformation of the basic tenants of the Soviet system.

The fall-out of the 'Thaw' was felt almost immediately. Revolts in both Poland and Hungary demonstrated the limits of reform. Within the Soviet Union itself, authorities had to contend with popular unrest. On June 2nd, 1962, local workers seized both the Communist party headquarters and the police station in the Georgian city of Novocherkassk.[15] The workers were demanding cheaper food prices, better working conditions, and finally additional political reforms. This small-scale revolt was brutally put down by the authorities. Regular Soviet troops were called in to restore order, killing 16 protesters and injuring many more. Clearly any open dissent would not be tolerated. Rather the pace and content of reform was to be 'stage managed' by the state.

As troubling as these open acts of resistance were, the Soviet regime was equally concerned with a much more prevalent challenge to their authority. By the early sixties, authorities had noticed a disconcerting trend developing amongst young people. This 'Thaw' generation,[16] seemed to lack the combination of persuasive fear and intense nationalism that had helped motivate conformity during the Stalin era. A public survey conducted by the state in 1964 revealed that four out of every five university students refused to participate in various Soviet mass mobilization projects, including the 'Virgin Lands' campaign.[17] As the proceeding decades would show, the unfulfilled promises of the Khrushchev era reforms would not further bind the population with the regime. Rather, the exact opposite would be the case. Ordinary citizens, particularly young people, increasingly withdrew from politics. Both the fear and genuine enthusiasm of the Stalin era simply disappeared.[18] A slow and steady rot had begun. This rot would ultimately prove too much for the Soviet system to counter during the crisis decade of the 1980s, despite the best intentions of a new generation of Soviet reformers.

CONCLUSION

When assessing the place of the Khrushchev era reforms in the larger context both Soviet and global history, one needs to consider the importance of the Stalin Revolution. Like it or not, 'Soviet civilization' was ultimately forged during the Stalin period. By both opening up the system to popular criticism and questioning the legacy of many of the Soviet Union's foundational myths, the Khrushchev regime unwittingly unleashed powerful forces that they quite simply could not control. Although Khrushchev's successors attempted to undo many of the post-1956 reforms, the genie could not be put back into the bottle. By the time Mikhail Gorbachev also tried to strengthen and protect the Soviet-style system through limited reform, the damage was already done. In this sense, one needs to see February 1956 as the logical precursor to August 1991.

QUESTIONS FOR FURTHER DISCUSSION

- According to Khrushchev, what were (Be specific) Stalin's major crimes? How did these crimes contradict or deviate from Leninism? In your opinion, which of these Stalinist offenses does Khrushchev consider the most important?

- At the heart of Khrushchev's critique of the Stalin system is the idea that Marxism can indeed be reformed or revised. Using your reading of the text and other course readings, make a case for or against a 'revisionist' model of Marxism.

NOTES

1. The best of the recent examples of this is Vladislav Zubok's *A Failed Empire: The Soviet Union in the Cold War from Stalin to Gorbachev* (Chapel Hill: UNC Press, 2009).

2. See both Alexei Yurchak, *Everything was Forever, Until it was No More: The Last Soviet Generation* (Princeton: Princeton University Press, 2006), and Sergei Zhuk, *Rock and Roll in the Rocket City: The West, Identity, and Ideology in Soviet Dniepropetrovsk, 1960–1985* (Washington DC: Woodrow Wilson Center Press, 2010).

3. Although Khrushchev himself was dismissed by the CPSU's conservative wing in 1964, vestiges of the 'Thaw' lasted into the early Brezhnev era and beyond. For our purposes, we will designate the crushing of the Prague Spring in 1968 and subsequent KGB crack-down on Soviet dissents as our cap date.

4. These include Moshe Lewin who contends that the Stalin revolution created "a highly bureaucratized 'statist' system." In Moshe Lewin, *The Making of the Soviet System: Essays in the Social History of Interwar Russia* (New York: Pantheon, 1985). Similar readings of the Stalin system can be found in the writings of Lev Trotsky during his exile period 1929–1941.

5. For more on Stalinist 'mass culture' see truly the excellent monograph, *Cultivating the Masses: Modern State Practices and Soviet Socialism, 1914–1939* (Ithaca: Cornell University Press, 2011) by David L. Hoffmann.

6. Stephen Kotkin, *Magnetic Mountain: Stalinism as Civilization* (Berkley: University of California Press, 1995), 5–6.

7. See Shelia Fitzpatrick, *Education and Social Mobility in the Soviet Union, 1921–1934* (Cambridge: Cambridge University Press, 1979).

8. Kotkin, 6–7.

9. Josip Broz Tito's Yugoslavia is the obvious exception to this Stalinist orthodoxy; however, it was only after the 1948 Soviet-Yugoslavia that the regime took any concrete steps to break with the Stalinist model. Indeed, many facets of the Stalinist model (emphasis on heavy industrial development, etc.) remained key features of the Yugoslavian system throughout the Cold War.

10. Nikita Khrushchev, "Special Report to the 20th Congress of the CSPU, February 24–25, 1956."

11. Suri, Jeremi. "The Rise and Fall of an International Counterculture, 1960–1975." *American Historical Review,* 114. 1 (February 2009), 54.

12. Alexander Prokhov, "Cinema of the Thaw 1953–1967" in *The Russian Cinema Reader: Volume Two, The Thaw to the Present* (Boston: Academic Studies Press, 2013), 14–17.

13. *Ibid.,*19.

14. Susan Reid, "Cold War in the Kitchen: Gender and the De-Stalinization of Consumer Taste in the Soviet Union under Khrushchev," *Slavic Review* 61, no. 2 (2002), 242.

15. Jeremi Suri, "The Promise and Failure of 'Developed Socialism': The Soviet 'Thaw' and the Crucible of the Prague Spring, 1964–1972," in *Contemporary European History,* 15, no. 2 (May 2003), 133–158.

16. The best single work on these events is Samuel H. Baron's *Bloody Sunday in the Soviet Union: Novocherkassk, 1962* (Stanford: Stanford University Press, 2001).

17. For more on this 'Thaw' Generation see both Vladioslav Zubok's *Zhivago's Children* (Cambridge: Harvard University Press, 2009) and Donald Raleigh's *Soviet Baby Boomers* (London: Oxford University Press, 2001).

18. Jeremi Suri, "The Rise and Fall of an International Counterculture, 1960–1975," 50.

BIBLIOGRAPHY/SUGGESTED READINGS

Hornsby, Robert. *Protest, Reform, and Repression in Khrushchev's Soviet Union.* Cambridge: Cambridge University Press, 2013.

Kotkin, Stephen. *Magnetic Mountain: Stalinism as Civilization.* Berkley: University of California Press, 1995.

Raleigh, Donald. *Russia's Sputnik Generation: Soviet Baby Boomers Talk about Their Lives.* Bloomington: Indiana University Press, 2006.

Yurachak, Alexei. *Everything Was Forever, until it was No More: The Last Soviet Generation.* Princeton: Princeton University Press, 2006.

Zubok, Vladislav. *A Failed Empire: The Soviet Union in the Cold War from Stalin to Gorbachev.* Chapel Hill: University of North Carolina Press, 2007.

----------------, *Zhivago's Children: The Last Russian Intelligentsia.* Cambridge: Harvard University Press, 2009.

CHAPTER III

Individualism and Nationalism

Unity and Division: The Questions for Early American Constitutions

Joseph Myers

The better to secure and perpetuate mutual friendship and intercourse among the people of the different States in this Union, the free inhabitants of each of these States, paupers, vagabonds, and fugitives from justice excepted, shall be entitled to all privileges and immunities of free citizens in the several States; and the people of each State shall free ingress and regress to and from any other State, and shall enjoy therein all the privileges of trade and commerce, subject to the same duties, impositions, and restrictions as the inhabitants thereof respectively, provided that such restrictions shall not extend so far as to prevent the removal of property imported into any State, to any other State, of which the owner is an inhabitant; provided also that no imposition, duties or restriction shall be laid by any State, on the property of the United States, or either of them. If any person guilty of, or charged with, treason, felony, or other high misdemeanor in any State, shall flee from justice, and be found in any of the United States, he shall, upon demand of the Governor or executive power of the State from which he fled, be delivered up and removed to the State having jurisdiction of his offense. . . . The United States in Congress assembled shall never engage in a war, nor grant letters of marque or reprisal in time of peace, nor enter into any treaties or alliances, nor coin money, nor regulate the value thereof, nor ascertain the sums and expenses necessary for the defense and welfare of the United States, or any of them, nor emit bills, nor borrow money on the credit of the United States, nor appropriate money, nor agree upon the number of vessels of war, to be built or purchased, or the number of land or sea forces to be raised, nor appoint a commander in chief of the army or navy, unless nine States assent to the same: nor shall a question on any other point, except for adjourning from day to day be determined, unless by the votes of the majority of the United States in Congress assembled.

—Articles of Confederation, 1777

In the United States we now have a written constitution of government that outlines the specific legislative, executive and judicial functions, as well as other things, of the Federal Government. But just because that is what we have now does not mean that all governments have constitutions like ours, or even that the United States always had the same type of constitutional system. The British Empire at the time of the American Revolution also had a constitution, but it wasn't embodied in any one document. Instead the British Constitution was hundreds of documents—laws and traditions that were established over centuries. Most of all the British Constitution was a balance of social classes in the British Empire. There were three social classes, the Kings and Queens (they were a social class by themselves), the nobility (called the Lords) and everyone else (called the commons). Over time the Commons became represented by a House of Commons, which was a body of representatives that represented the interests of all who were common by birth in the Empire—everyone who was common was represented whether they were a farmer in Wales, a shopkeeper in London, or a cobbler in Boston. Even the slaves in the colonies were represented by the House of Commons in the British Constitution, because your blood determined your representation, not any voting rights. It was blood succession that determined who was king. Nobles were born noble and Commons were born common. And the balance of King, Lords and Commons making, executing and defining law is what defined the British Constitution.

Congress Hall in Philadelphia

© Roman Babakin/Shutterstock.com

In the British Colonies of North America, however, that blood based representation created a problem. The colonists were all common. There were no nobles living in the colonies and the King lived in England several thousand miles away. So colonial governments that handled local affairs were all controlled by the commons in each of the colonies. By the dawn of the American Revolution most British colonists came to believe that "their government" was their individual colonial government that was mostly chosen by the free voters of each colony. In America representation became equated by voting instead of blood. And there you have it. Voting versus blood became one of the main factors in the conflict that caused the American Revolution.

Even before independence was declared by the colonies in July 1776, the leaders of the Revolution in the Continental Congress began thinking about constitutions and constitutional forms. One thing they all agreed upon was that the governments in each colony, soon to be called states, were the only government they thought that should make, execute and define law over the citizens of each new state. New states needed state constitutions to define how each state determined making, executing and defining law, but no one brought up the idea that there needed to be one constitution

The Signing of the Declaration of Independence in 1776

for the whole new United States, because no one yet thought of the United States as one big country. These Founding Fathers did realize that to get their independence they needed a unity of all the states and that had to be defined. In January of 1776, 7 months before independence they made a plan to first get allies, then unite in a formal confederation and then declare independence.

SIGNING OF THE DECLARATION OF INDEPENDENCE

British war legislation and a new British army that was sent to North America in the Spring of 1776 changed all that. The timetable was altered and so in May of 1776 the Continental Congress authorized the colonies to redefine government as based on the people instead of the King. State Constitutions were needed but no Federal. The plan of union which became known as the Articles of Confederation was first submitted as a draft to the whole of Congress in August of 1776 and would not be fully worked out until November of 1777 when it was finally sent to the states for ratification. The Articles are often referred to as the first constitution of the United States, but part of the reason we think that is because of the Constitution of 1787 and what that document came to mean. The Articles was at best a part of the overall constitution of the states. Much like the British Constitution which was made up of many laws and documents, the "Constitution" of the states included several things—the state constitutions and the agreement of unity, the Articles of Confederation—not one document, but several. And why wouldn't the "original constitution" follow the conception of the British Constitution and be composed of many things. After all, the Founding Fathers were British, both by the culture they had grown up in and by ethnicity. The leaders of the

Revolution were British and they lived in separate British colonies, and that is how they went about framing the United States and any government for those states.

So if the colonies were separate, almost like separate countries, it would seem that the "original constitution" would state that. What do the Articles indicate on that point? The first of the Articles deals with just that, the states are determined as separate and independent, as if they were 13 separate and independent nations. After stating the separateness of the states the Articles then defines under what circumstance these separate nations would act in unity. This system was very different from what we now recognize as "one nation," and why would it have been any different? The colonies were separate colonies. The only commonality, the only unity the colonies ever knew was that they were all British colonies (and most of the free people in those colonies were ethnically British). But things changed. War and Revolution have a way of doing that.

After serving in the "Continental" Army or the "Continental" Congress, some of the Revolutionaries came to identify with the group of states, the "continent," as a whole instead of just their home state. These revolutionaries began to think of unity before separateness. They began to see themselves through the course of the Revolutionary War as American more than they did as being from their "separate and independent" state. The two most important of these figures were James Madison and George Washington.

After the War Madison and Washington exchanged several letters where they wrote about how disappointed they were in the separation of the states and the limited unity of the states. Madison proposed that the arrangement of the Articles had to be changed to form one country. He got support from Washington who fought in the worst conditions for 8 years on behalf of the "continent" and not just for Virginia, his home state. Madison got the southern states and Pennsylvania to send delegates to a convention in Annapolis, Maryland, in 1786. The convention was supposed to be a forum to talk about economic matters between the states but Madison got the delegates to recommend altering the Articles of Confederation. He got his wish and the Continental Congress authorized a convention to meet in May of 1787 in Philadelphia to alter and amend the Articles of Confederation. George Washington just happened to be in town for a convention of officers from the "Continental" Army. Nice how that worked out. So Washington was able to be at the convention who chose him to be the presiding officer, president, over the convention's proceedings.

But Madison didn't want to alter or amend the Articles. He brought with him a draft of a proposed Constitution which would form one government over all of the states. Such a plan of a central authority would not have been possible in 1776. Remember, the Revolution was based on the idea that no one government, like the British Parliament, could make, execute and define law over the citizens of any colony. Look into the Articles. Does any article give the power to legislate to the Continental Congress? Could the Continental Congress tax the new states under the Articles? The Continental Congress could provide services to the states—organize a military, print money, make treaties, send ambassadors—but it could not make, execute and define law over the citizens of each new state or over the governments of those states. If the Continental Congress wanted money, it could only request money from the states, but it could not make a law to tax the states or the citizens of the states. And that lack of power nearly cost the Revolution because the states very seldom gave the Continental Congress the money it requested. Madison knew that the "Continent" could not remain independent with a system where unity came after separation.

QUESTIONS FOR FURTHER DISCUSSION

- What does the Articles say about legislative power? How is that different from Article I of the Constitution of 1787?

- The Articles of Confederation are most similar to which of the Articles in the Constitution of 1787? Does the Continental Congress under the Articles of Confederation seem more similar to Congress under Article I of the Constitution of 1787 or the executive branch as defined by Article II?

- What makes an "American Government"? Decide what the differences are between the Continental Congress as a body of unity, and the framework of legislative, executive and judicial in the Constitution of 1787.

- Would you classify the Articles of Confederation as "a" constitution, and the continental Congress as "the" government of the United States, after looking at these two documents?

BIBLIOGRAPHY/SUGGESTED READINGS

Butler, Jon. *Becoming America: The Revolution before 1776* (Cambridge: Harvard Univ. Press, 2000).

Doll, Peter M. *Revolution, Religion and National Identity* (Madison, N.J.: Farleigh Dickinson Univ. Press, 2000).

Landsman, Ned C. *From Colonials to Provincials: American Thought and Culture* (Boston: Twayne Publishers, 1997).

Marston, Jerrilyn Greene. *King and Congress: The Transfer of Political Legitimacy from the King to the Continental Congress, 1774–1776* (Princeton, 1987).

Rakove, Jack. *The Beginnings of National Politics: An Interpretive History of the Continental Congress* (New York: Alfred A. Knopf, 1979).

Freedom:
Comparing Visions of Community and Individuality

Joseph Myers

Any crossing of two beings not at exactly the same level produces a medium between the level of the two parents. This means: the offspring will probably stand higher than the racially lower parent, but not as high as the higher one. Consequently, it will later succumb in the struggle against the higher level. Such mating is contrary to the will of Nature for a higher breeding of all life. The precondition for this does not lie in associating superior and inferior, but in the total victory of the former. The stronger must dominate and not blend with the weaker, thus sacrificing his own greatness. Only the born weakling can view this as cruel, but he after all is only a weak and limited man; for if this law did not prevail, any conceivable higher development of organic living beings would be unthinkable.

—Adolph Hitler, *Mein Kampf*, 1925

In the future days, which we seek to make secure, we look forward to a world founded upon four essential human freedoms. The first is freedom of speech and expression—everywhere in the world. The second is freedom of every person to worship God in his own way—everywhere in the world. The third is freedom from want, which, translated into world terms, means economic understandings which will secure to every nation a healthy peacetime life for its inhabitants—everywhere in the world. The fourth is freedom from fear, which, translated into world terms, means a world-wide reduction of armaments to such a point and in such a thorough fashion that no nation will be in a position to commit an act of physical aggression against any neighbor—anywhere in the world.

—Franklin Roosevelt, *The Four Freedoms*, 1941

n American culture freedom is a concept that is often discussed but seldom defined. We think we know what it means so we don't need to think about what it means, or what it has meant at different times or in different places. Most students of history would agree that World War II was about freedom, but what they do not realize is that both the Allies and the United States, and Nazi Germany and the Axis Powers, both fought for freedom. The notions of freedom, the understanding of rights and what it meant to be human, however, were different for these two conflicting sides. In the readings from "The Four Freedoms," by U.S. President Franklin Roosevelt in 1940, and "Nation and Race," a chapter from Adolph Hitler's *Mein Kampf*, two very different definitions of freedom emerge, which shows the difference between societies that see humans as a function of their personal qualities and individuality, and societies that view the individual as a function of the group to which they belong.

Notions of freedom are not only different across historical time, but also vary from place to place within the same time period. Differences are based primarily on the value structure of that society—not the institutional structures, but the values that inform those institutions. What does that mean? It means that two separate countries appearing at the same time or different times can be democracies but not have the same definition of freedom. Both democracies, the institution of government, but a different value system when it comes to defining what democracy means. And believe it or not, Nazi Germany began as a democracy. Oh, very different from the way you would define it, more than likely, but with an elected executive, a popularly elected national legislature, and a constitutional structure agreed upon by the people. Things changed but democratic it was nonetheless. Hitler defined German democracy as having the people choose the party or person who had the best idea for Germany and then giving that party or person full power to realize that idea. That's not like American Democracy, but it is institutionally democracy. So what is the difference? The values behind what the institutional form is supposed to enact, and the rationale behind why government has power in the first place.

Elsewhere in this reader, Fascism has been defined basically as a system that promoted group values, and in terms of Nazi Germany your reading in this section shows you how Hitler articulated what that meant in terms of freedom. In this section the point of what Hitler is saying is to define the basis of freedom within the context of a racial group, and that the freedom of that racial group, the Germans, or as the Nazis called them, Aryans, was the only important thing that a government was supposed to promote. Individuality, individual rights, individual worth meant very little in this ideology. Group meant everything, individual meant nothing. To an American in the 21st century the notion that freedom is about a racial group not being affected by any other racial group should appear odd, or at least at odds with the principles of the United States—and it is! It is if you are in America in the 21st century, but Nazi ideas about freedom are not that odd from a historical perspective. Instead the value structure of Nazi Germany is what is most often seen in the last 5,000 years of civilization. "My group is the best, and to make it free, truly free, we need to make sure no other group influences what we do." Hitler didn't say that but he may as well have . . . along with countless other empires, kingdoms, countries, nations, city-states and whatever sort of institutional framework humans have devised.

The values informing the United States' institutional framework of democracy are different than Nazi Germany, though sometimes in practice the US has been closer to Nazi Germany than you might think. The American definition of freedom, as articulated in the Declaration of Independence and institutionalized in the governmental framework of the Constitution, is meant to promote individuality and individual pursuits through a recognition that society believes that all individuals have rights and that they have inherent worth. The basis of society, and therefore its greatest value, is on the individual's right to self-definition and self-determination. The individual is important and, therefore, the group is better off when it promotes individual expression and protects the rights of individuals. "An individual is important and to be free, truly free, we need to make sure that each individual can define their own lives and determine their own actions without regard to what group they are in—and that makes our whole group better for our members." Franklin Roosevelt didn't say that but he may as well have . . . and very few countries have ever had that value system. Even in the world we live in the 21st century, most cultures reject the idea that all individuals should be free to define their own lives. The values of the United States are not the norm; that would be Nazi Germany.

So let's break down these readings to help you see where these two leaders were so different, and their countries fought a war to promote two very different visions of freedom.

"NATION AND RACE" FROM *MEIN KAMPF*

The book *Mein Kampf* was published first in 1925, just after Adolph Hitler was released from prison where he served a short term for treason—he tried to forcefully take over the German government in 1923 and it failed miserably. The title means "My Struggle." The book is a sweeping picture of his life, his service to Germany in World War I and how he believed Germany could rebound from its defeat in that war. Most intellectuals in Germany dismissed the book as unsystematic rantings, which pandered to an unsophisticated audience. The book sold around twenty thousand copies in its initial printing, but as the Nazi party grew in the late 1920s and early 1930s sales picked up and Hitler's vision began to strike a chord with a German population that wanted to return to the glory days of the German Empire. When Hitler became Chancellor (prime minister) of Germany after the Nazi Party took control of the German Reichstag (legislature) in 1933, steps were taken to put all power into his hands so that the value system

Adolph Hitler in 1923

© Roman Nerud/Shutterstock.com

indicated in "Nation and Race" could be enacted. So what was that value system?

Notice where Hitler starts this section—he starts out in Nature, but this is not the "Nature and Nature's God" indicated in the Declaration of Independence during the American Revolution that was based on Enlightenment rationalism—this is nature without reason. Hitler starts his line of thinking from a place of "common sense," which appeals to the idea of what you see is true, and therefore just asks his reader to look simply at things on the surface. This simplistic approach brings him to a very simple conclusion that nature really has determined that "blood" is the defining element of being. And what does that mean? It means that all beings are defined by the blood they are born with and that nature intended that beings with different blood look out for their own interests and never mix that blood. What this means in human terms is that different races and different ethnicities are different blood groups and they should never mix. While this separation of blood does not totally define freedom, Hitler is stating that separation is implicitly necessary to realize freedom.

What the argument about blood also means is that Hitler is defining individuality in terms of being part of a group. Within that context Nazi ideology defines 3 types of human groupings, all defined, not by their actions, but by their blood: Culture Founders, Culture Bearers and Culture Destroyers. The Aryans (Germanic peoples of northern and western Europe) are the Founders of Culture and therefore the Master Race. In "Nation and Race" Hitler doesn't really deal with the Bearers much and instead spends most of the chapter talking about the number one culture destroyer as he sees it, Jews. The chapter establishes the difference between the Aryan and the Jew, which is defined by blood (by a person's DNA). In the context of this chapter, Hitler uses "Jew" as a term that is both literal and figurative: literally the Nazis perceived a threat to German freedom from the Jews, but also figuratively because "Jews" represented the traits of all culture destroyers, who needed to be, by Nazi Ideology, destroyed. The rationale for why Germans and the Aryans are masters is an inherent trait to their blood, and likewise Jews are destroyers because they are born that way—both groups and all individuals of that group bear the same qualities because it is part of their biology, and so you can't change who or what you are by choices. That means this Nazi ideology is not a rational ideology, but an irrational one. A person is evaluated not on the choices they make and the outcome of their actions, but instead by blood, by what group you belong to. That's why all Germans are good, and all Jews are bad according to Hitler. To Hitler individual choices or expressions do not define a person, only what group they belong to by blood defines them. If you were Jewish, it wouldn't matter that you had a great personality, or were boring, whether you were smart or stupid. Those qualities don't define you, only blood does, and for that reason, Hitler asserts, the Aryan must protect their Nation from other groups and from other blood. Protection of the group from outside influence is the only important goal of government and society—freedom, Nazi style.

Further, note the rationale that Hitler establishes as to why the Founder is good and the destroyer so bad; it's because the Aryan Founder is able to suppress individual desire for the good of the group—to think in terms of the group first. To Hitler what makes Jews as a group so destructive is that they protect their individual needs. Here is kind of a paradox: The Destroyers are a bad group because the members of the group can only think of individual interests. Group good, individual bad.

"FOUR FREEDOMS" FROM FRANKLIN ROOSEVELT

Franklin Roosevelt was first elected to the Presidency of the United States in 1932, and he would be re-elected in 1936 and 1940 before making the "Four Freedoms" Speech to Congress in early 1941 at the beginning of his 3rd term in office. No one has been President longer than Franklin Roosevelt and since the ratification of the 22nd Amendment in 1951 Presidents can now only serve 2 terms. Yet being elected President 4 times (he also won re-election in 1944) was not the biggest innovation Roosevelt (sometimes referred to by his initials FDR) was known for. What Roosevelt's policies, called the New Deal, was to make the Federal Government more interactive with individual citizens in a way only the States were before his election. In some ways, historians have argued, this changed the nature of American democracy to link the rights of citizens more directly to the nation than to the states, and therefore changing the value structure of democracy in the United States. In the "Four Freedoms," Roosevelt articulates the value system of the United States that was just about to go to war with Nazi Germany. So how was that value system articulated?

Roosevelt begins his speech by defining the nation and its obligation to protect the group and other similar democratic groups. The rationale for going to war was pretty simple for Roosevelt; the democratic values of the United States and other similar democracies were threatened by the Fascist system of Nazi Germany and its allies. If the United States did not enter World War II sooner rather than later, America might find itself alone in trying to fight the Axis Powers. Roosevelt notes that the United States does not enter into war lightly, and really seldom had in its history—here he implies that the goal of the United States is different from other nations in that here individuals live their own lives not lives of conquest on behalf of the group. The American population historically had only favored military action when directly attacked, and this speech is delivered before Pearl Harbor, in part to get Americans ready for the war that Roosevelt believes the nation will soon fight.

The Franklin Roosevelt Memorial in Washington, DC

In readying a nation for war, Roosevelt outlines what he believes the national policy should be. And notice that in stating the specifics of this policy strategy, Roosevelt begins with the phrase, "by an impressive expression of the public will." Roosevelt is targeting the group, not individuals, but what the group will need to do to protect its freedom. Is this a form of group freedom similar to Nazi Germany? After all, it needs to be remembered that the United States had certain structures similar to that of Nazi Germany. The Nuremberg Laws of Nazi Germany that denied many rights and public services to Jews and non-Aryans were very similar to Jim Crow Laws and other segregation practices found not just in the southern States but most everywhere in the United States since the end of the Civil War. The biggest difference between the United States and Nazi Germany was that the Federal Government of the United States did not develop a system of extermination for minority groups the way the Nazis did, but even the Federal Government practiced discrimination with measures like the segregation of the Armed Forces. The problem with the discriminatory racial policy in the United States was that the values of America were supposed to promote an equal freedom for all individuals, unlike in Nazi Germany where both values and policy supported each other in persecuting minority groups. Roosevelt's speech ends with an acknowledgment to the goal of an individualized freedom that the United States has always tried to perfect, even when policies used group segregation to deny freedom.

The Four Freedoms are listed rather simply and without much commentary. Roosevelt defines freedom not from a group context but through what an individual can do and be. Self-definition and self-determination, choice, are the basis of each of the Four Freedoms. Notice even the second freedom, which is not listed as freedom of religion, but freedom "to worship God in his own way." This freedom is not linked to a group religious practice but to the individual's spiritual understanding. And that is essentially the same logic for the value system in all of the freedoms Roosevelt defines as freedom in America. The freedom of the individual defines the freedom of the group.

QUESTIONS FOR FURTHER DISCUSSION

- Why is racial purity at the core of Hitler's development of his ideology of Aryan Supremacy?

- If freedom in America is supposed to protect all individuals then why do race, gender and other forms of group discrimination exist?

- Do you think it was easy or difficult for Germans to accept Hitler's argument on Race? Do you think it would be hard for Americans to accept it? Why or why not?

- Why doesn't Roosevelt address race or gender or other group definitions in developing his understanding of the United States entry into World War II?

BIBLIOGRAPHY/SUGGESTED READINGS

Kazin, Michael, and Joseph A. McCartin, eds. *Americanism: New Perspectives on the History of an Ideal* (Univ. of North Carolina Press, 2012).

Nicosia, Francis R., and David Scrase, eds. *Jewish Life in Nazi Germany* (Berghahn Books, 2013).

Decolonization:
The Fall of the British Empire,
1945–1980

James Esposito

In the twentieth century, and especially since the end of the war, the processes which gave birth to the nation states of Europe have been repeated all over the world. We have seen the awakening of national consciousness in peoples who have for centuries lived in dependence upon some other power. Fifteen years ago this movement spread through Asia. Many countries there, of different races and civilizations, pressed their claim to an independent national life. Today the same thing is happening in Africa, and the most striking of all the impressions that I have formed since I left London a month ago is of the strength of this African national consciousness. In different places it takes different forms, but it is happening everywhere. The wind of change is blowing through this continent and whether we like it or not, this growth of national consciousness is a political fact. And we must all accept it as a fact, and our national policies must take account of it.

—Harold Macmillan, *Winds of Change Speech*, 1960

INTRODUCTION

Britain's place as a worldwide colonial empire began to decline in the years immediately following the World War Two. Victory over Nazi Germany and Imperial Japan felt like a pyrrhic one: Britain faced food rationing, extensive bomb damage, and bankruptcy. Britain had led the war against fascism in 1939, only to end the conflict as a junior partner to the United States. At the same time, the British Empire had grown to gargantuan proportions with colonies or protectorates occupying large swaths of the Middle East, Asia, and Africa. Britain's enlarged empire greatly outstripped the resources and political will to maintain a presence everywhere.

The nationalist movement in India under Mahatma Gandhi, Jawaharlal Nehru, and the Congress Party had grown in strength during the interwar period. Limited home rule was granted through the Government of India Act in 1935. Full independence was granted under great political pressure in 1947.[1] India and Pakistan were formally separated on religious lines and the British colonial service members returned home. Despite this setback, the postwar years marked a high point in hope and optimism for imperial reform.[2]

Kenya, Rhodesia, Nigeria, and Ghana were thought to be too underdeveloped for national independence until the 1970s or even later. Unlike India, with its strong civil service, state, and military organization, the British Empire in Africa was quite dispersed, with the colonial state operating through tribal networks and white settler communities. Southern Africa in particular had a large white settler population. The British government had supported the emigration of former servicemen to build farmsteads in South Africa, Kenya, and Rhodesia.[3] The settler class was intended to be a permanent fixture of life in Anglophone Africa, maintaining the authority of the colonial state in the name of white supremacy and extracting the economic value of large agricultural, mineral, and labor resources of the region. Britain's settler colonies would supply cheap raw materials, food, and other commodities in exchange for finished products manufactured by the imperial center.

NKRUMAH, SETTLER COLONIALISM, AND THE "WINDS OF CHANGE"

Ghanaian leader Kwame Nkrumah, inspired by Gandhi and the Congress Party in India, moved for national independence in the shortest possible time. By 1957, Nkrumah would declare himself president of the Gold Coast and by 1960 he declared an independent Republic of Ghana. Unlike Southern Africa, the Gold Coast had been occupied but not heavily settled by British. A hub of the slave trade and then gold extraction in the nineteenth century, Ghana's natural

Kwame Nkrumah

resources made it a useful, albeit unessential colonial asset by the 1950s. Nevertheless, Nkrumah's example was an important moment for African identity—self-rule was not only possible, but could happen almost immediately.

Kenya, on the other hand, was the site of an important confrontation between Mau Mau guerrillas and British Army forces. The Kikuyu people deeply resented British settlement and farming of the White Highlands region. A center of British settler life and economic engine of the colony, the Kikuyu were forcibly removed from their ancestral lands in favor of British agricultural interests.[4] Faced with the prospect of marginal existence as squatters or casual labors on European estates, the Kikuyu rebelled in what was known as the Mau Mau Uprising.

In 1952, the Mau Mau organized several attacks on European members of the colony. Prominent tribal chiefs and white settlers were ambushed and killed in a series of assassinations. In order to defeat the growing movement, the colonial administration attempted to capture and imprison important members of the organization during a massive crackdown in 1954. The colonial government in Nairobi interned thousands of Kikuyu, rushed land reform, and placed Kikuyu families in "protected villages" under military control. Thousands died directly and indirectly as a result of counter-insurgency tactics employed by the British military and settler government.[5] Evelyn Baring, governor of Kenya, was concerned that anything less than total destruction of the Mau Mau would cause the colonial government to collapse. Sensationalized depictions of assassinations of white colonists were used to justify harsh measures to crush the insurgency.

By 1960, the British had given up on their minority rule position in Kenya. Despite years of fighting, the costs of minority rule as well as the negative attention received by the international community forced the colonial government to embrace decolonization. African participation in government led to national independence under the Kenya leader Jomo Kenyatta in 1963. Newly freed from prison, Kenyatta led Kenya through the 1960s and 1970s. Kenyatta redistributed large landholdings once held by British settlers and provided a moderate leadership for the national economic development.

Prime Minister Harold Macmillan's speech to the South African parliament clarified the British position on formal empire and white minority rule. While South Africa had a large number of British settlers who worked in farms, mining, or industry, the largest population of Europeans were Afrikaners. Afrikaners, descendants of Dutch colonists in the seventeenth and eighteenth centuries, had imposed a rigid racial divide in South Africa during the nineteenth and early twentieth century. Blacks were not allowed to live in the same neighborhoods or cities as whites, had inferior local government and educational systems, and were barred from holding property in white areas.[6] The black majority population was well aware of developments going on throughout Africa and demanded majority rule just as Ghana and Kenya had done.

Macmillan made clear that the era of minority rule was ending in Africa, and white South Africans would have to embrace their black neighbors for a share in government. Anything less would jeopardize the security and reputation of South Africa as a member of the democratic West, likely leading its black population to seek assistance from the Soviet Union. Learning from the Suez Crisis, a military intervention against nationalist government in Egypt in 1956 and experience with anticolonial insurgencies in Kenya and Malaya Emergency, Macmillan pleaded for South Africa to accept majority rule, or risk civil war against communist-aligned rebels.

"Winds of Change" prompted Prime Minister Hendrik Verwoerd to formally institute Apartheid, the racialized system of separation and marginalization of blacks in South Africa.[7] Macmillan warned that Apartheid would lead to a boycott of South African goods in Britain and the United States. Government sanctioned separation simply would not be compatible with the global politics of the late twentieth century. Despite this, Macmillan remained sensitive to the position of white South Africans. Decolonization had showed that white control of land and resources would likely be turned over to black inhabitants through land retribution or nationalization valuable infrastructure like the Suez Canal. South Africa's large farms and valuable natural resources risked seizure. Many postcolonial states compelled their white inhabitants to emigrate after decolonization, leaving a strong sense of anxiety and danger amongst white Africans.

Blacks in South Africa lived under appalling conditions. They were forced into "townships," ghettos that ringed many of the major cities. Townships were a means to concentrate and control blacks into separate communities. The Pass Laws required blacks to have special identity papers to work in cities like Johannesburg or Pretoria during the day time and return home at night. They were also assigned dangerous jobs like diamond mining or menial ones like farm labor for substandard wages, impoverishing and disempowering them in their own country. The South African military and police mobilized to control these subject populations, utilizing many of the techniques of divide and rule borrowed from the British. Apartheid state employed violence and intimidation tactics to intimidate and terrorize black Africans.[8] Prominent opposition leaders like Nelson Mandela were imprisoned, killed, or simply "disappeared."

After Macmillan's speech, South Africa took radical measures to split up the population into distinct ethnic groups, disenfranchise black voters, and make any organized native African or communist associations a criminal offense. Throughout the years South African officials would cloak their racist policies in the language of "anticommunism." Any act seen to compromise the Apartheid state could be construed to be communist infiltration, complicating the geopolitical position of the United States and Great Britain with South Africa.

Despite the odious reputation of the Apartheid regime, the United States and Great Britain had difficulty abandoning South Africa entirely. The United States sought an ally in the global Cold War, one which could be called upon to intervene in sub-Saharan Africa, a region of the world that the Soviet Union had success pulling towards the communist bloc. The United States also had significant trade and investment in South Africa, which included subsidies of major US corporations, uranium mining,

Henrik Verwoerd

and precious metals extraction.[9] The United Kingdom was also hesitant to abandon South Africa as an ally and trading partner. South Africa was home to a large English-speaking diaspora with access to resources and infrastructure developed by British firms in the early twentieth century.[10] Both nations did not formally disassociate themselves with Apartheid South Africa until the 1980s. With mounting domestic and international pressure, the regime collapsed in 1994.

"WINDRUSH" AND MULTICULTURALISM

Decolonization opened up multicultural life in the United Kingdom. In 1948, the *Empire Windrush* arrived in Tilbury, near London with the first generation of Jamaican immigrants. This first transport ship started a wave of West Indian and Asian immigration which started to transform the demographic and cultural makeup of the British Isles. Postwar economic growth and labor shortage encouraged immigrants to start a new life in Britain.

Multiculturalism was challenged from its inception. The British government struggled to formulate a coherent policy for new black and Asian populations. Some in government had planned to send the *Windrush* back to Jamaica, however due to the nature of citizenship laws in the Commonwealth and Empire, the new immigrants had a legal claim to British citizenship.[11] The British Nationality Act of 1948 gave full rights of entry and relocation to citizens of the Commonwealth. This had been established to ease white settler emigration to Canada and Australia as well as to encourage trade. It was not intended to encourage non-white immigration to Britain itself. Clement Attlee and his government were unable to formulate an argument against it without exposing an explicit racist bias. Facing a labor shortage and large numbers of Irish, Italian, and Polish immigrants, the policy was not changed.

New black immigrants were subject to threats and harassment. Many looked upon the arrivals with suspicion, and openly wondered how race would fit into Britain's class system. The working class, professional middle class, and the aristocracy had clashed throughout the nineteenth and twentieth century. The postwar period had secured a new social welfare state in which the government took a leading role in national economic development, attempting to smooth out the disparities of the interwar period. The welfare state was response to the privations and extremes of industrial capitalism of the previous half century. The state consolidated to promote economic growth, public healthcare, and social welfare benefits to its citizens.

Both Labour and Conservative governments worried about the implications of non-white immigration. Empire had not yet disappeared, and the government had planned for long-term occupation of African colonies. More importantly, the fundamental set of beliefs which underpinned empire remained intact long after formal empire ended. Many felt blacks were inferior to whites and were incapable of assimilation into British society. Whiteness was at the very core of the postwar welfare state just as racism was an essential component of empire. Black immigration fundamentally questioned what it meant to be British. Unlike class, it could not be disguised. Britishness is itself associated with the imperial project, as a fundamentally imagined group consciousness developed through the colonial encounter. If Britishness was defined as whiteness, as it was most often was, how could a black immigrant ever hope to become British?

The colonial project required a stark separation between the colonizer and colonized. Britain, as colonizer, would build institutions, extract resources, and force the colonized on the track towards modernity through education, native collaboration, and capitalist development. This was not an equal relationship nor was it simply 'exchange.' Immigration greatly complicated this as it showed blacks would have to be treated equally to their white counterparts as true British citizens. As empire came home new immigrants contended with attitudes and mentalities that were used to justify colonial domination. Many of these attitudes continued in society long after formal empire had ended. The postwar social science marked new black immigrants as inferior parents, poorer workers, and held cultural attitudes rearticulating older colonial mentalities as social intervention.[12] Perhaps more troubling, some were nostalgic for the "good old days" of empire and viewed multiculturalism as a kind of national trauma.[13]

Nevertheless, formal exclusion based on race was politically and socially unacceptable. The Second World War had shown how the "science" of race led to war and genocide—the Atlantic Charter and United Nations enshrined human rights as international law. The government eventually attempted to limit immigration to mostly skilled workers on the basis of the needs of the labor market. Multiculturalism was now the new path toward modernity for reluctant Britain, a nation that professed tolerance, freedom, and economic opportunity for all. Despite lingering prejudice, multiculturalism promised a new society and vision of the future for former imperial nation in decline.

CONCLUSION

A critical examination of decolonization shows how although Indian rule was ending, Britain believed it would rule large parts of Africa for the foreseeable future. Indian independence inspired Ghanaian and Kenyan independence movements, rapidly speeding up the process of decolonization. Macmillan's speech demonstrated that Britain would no longer intervene on the colonists' behalf. Decolonization also rapidly changed the demographic and cultural makeup of Britain itself. New immigrants, known as the *Windrush* Generation moved to the United Kingdom in large numbers challenging racial exclusion and notions of black inferiority, fundamental premises of the imperial project.

QUESTIONS FOR FURTHER DISCUSSION

- How did World War Two change the British Empire? What role did Indian independence play in decolonization?

- Who was Kwame Nkrumah? How did Ghanaian independence influence other national liberation movements in Kenya and elsewhere? How did the Mau Mau insurgency change attitudes towards empire in Britain?

- What did Macmillan mean by "winds of change"? How were white settler colonies different than Britain's colonies elsewhere? Why was South Africa important in the global Cold War?

- How did multiculturalism factor in to the decolonization narrative? What challenges did the *Windrush* Generation face when they arrived in Britain? Why was the British government hesitant to embrace immigration from its former empire?

NOTES

1. Mark Mazower, *No Enchanted Palace: The End of Empire and the Ideological Origins of the United Nations* (Princeton: Princeton University Press, 2013).

2. Wendy Webster calls the era from 1945 to Elizabeth II's 1953 coronation as the 'people's empire'—a kind of renewed hope manifested in popular film, newsreel, and radio of the period. This era also marked renewed scientific and military cooperation with Britain's colonies. See Wayne Renynold's *Australia's Bid for the Bomb* (2001).

3. Kathleen Paul, *Whitewashing Britain: Race and Citizenship in the Postwar Era* (Baltimore: Cornell University Press, 1997), 25.

4. Caroline Elkins, *Imperial Reckoning: The Untold Story of Britain's Gulag in Kenya* (New York: Holt, 2005).

5. Elkins, *Imperial Reckoning: The Untold Story of Britain's Gulag in Kenya*, 240–242.

6. Hermann Giliomee, "The Making of the Apartheid Plan, 1929–1948," *Journal of Southern African Studies* 29, no. 2 (June 2003), 377–380.

7. Ryan M. Irwin, *Gordian Knot: Apartheid and the Unmaking of the Liberal World Order* (New York: Oxford University Press, 2012) 20–27.

8. Nancy L. Clark and William H Worger, *South Africa: The Rise and Fall of Apartheid*, 2nd ed. (Harlow, England: Longman, 2011) 60–64.

9. Alex Thomson, *U.S. Foreign Policy Towards Apartheid South Africa, 1948–1994: Conflict of Interests* (New York, NY: Palgrave Macmillan, 2009), 21–23.

10. Peter J Schraeder, *United States Foreign Policy Toward Africa: Incrementalism, Crisis and Change* (Cambridge: Cambridge University Press, 1994), 195.

11. Kathleen Paul, *Whitewashing Britain: Race and Citizenship in the Postwar Era*, 134–135.

12. Jordana Bailkin, *Afterlife of Empire* (Berkeley: University of California Press, 2012).

13. Bill Schwarz, *Memories of Empire Volume 1: The White Man's World* (New York: Oxford University Press, 2011).

BIBLIOGRAPHY/SUGGESTED READINGS

Bailkin, Jordana. *Afterlife of Empire*. Berkeley: University of California Press, 2012.

Dubow, Saul. *Apartheid, 1948–1994*. Oxford, United Kingdom: Oxford University Press, 2014.

Elkins, Caroline. *Imperial Reckoning: The Untold Story of Britain's Gulag in Kenya*. New York: Holt, Henry & Company, 2005.

Fanon, Frantz, Richard Philcox, Jean-Paul Sartre, and Homi K Bhabha. *The Wretched of the Earth*. New York: Grove Press, 2005.

Mazower, Mark. *No Enchanted Palace: The End of Empire and the Ideological Origins of the United Nations*. Princeton, NJ, United States: Princeton University Press, 2013.

Paul, Kathleen. *Whitewashing Britain: Race and Citizenship in the Postwar Era*. Baltimore, MD, United States: Cornell University Press, 1997.

Webster, Wendy. *Englishness and Empire, 1939–1965*. New York: Oxford University Press, 2005.

CHAPTER IV

Spiritual Aspirations and Global Diversity

Swami Vivekananda, the *Bhagavad Gita*, and the 1893 World's Parliament of Religions

Jeffrey LaMonica

> We believe not only in universal toleration, but we accept all religions as true. . . . Sectarianism, bigotry, and its horrible descendant, fanaticism, have long possessed this beautiful earth. They have filled the earth with violence, drenched it often and often with human blood, destroyed civilization and sent whole nations to despair. Had it not been for these horrible demons, human society would be far more advanced than it is now. But their time is come; and I fervently hope that the bell that tolled this morning in honor of this convention may be the death-knell of all fanaticism, of all persecutions with the sword or with the pen, and of all uncharitable feelings between persons wending their way to the same goal.
>
> —Swami Vivekananda, *Welcome Address at the World's Parliament of Religions*, 1893

WORLD'S PARLIAMENT OF RELIGIONS, 1893

Spiritual leaders from ten different religious traditions gathered in Chicago, Illinois, in September 1893 for the first World's Parliament of Religions. This seventeen-day conference featured over two hundred speeches and proved to be the first step in the ongoing effort to establish and maintain religious tolerance and interreligious dialogue worldwide. Planning this international conversation began in 1890 with a group of Chicago Unitarians and Presbyterians led by Jenkin Lloyd Jones and John Henry Barrows. Jones, Barrows, and the General Commission of the Parliament of Religions decided to schedule the event in conjunction with the World's Colombian Exposition in Chicago in 1893. They invited religious speakers from around the world and established "universal peace" and "religious tolerance" as the Parliament's themes for discussion.[1]

Most of the Parliament's seven thousand attendees came to Chicago with a genuine interest in pursuing peace and tolerance. Some, however, were drawn by the opportunity to compare and contrast their theology with that of other faiths. For example, a large number of American Protestants used the Parliament to reinforce their belief in the inferiority of other religions. Furthermore, some religious leaders opposed the Parliament altogether. The General Assembly of the Presbyterian Church in the United States discouraged Barrows from organizing the event. Pope Leo XIII and the Archbishop of Canterbury Edward Benson criticized the conference and denounced the Catholics, including Cardinal James Gibbons, and Anglicans who attended. Sultan of the Ottoman Empire Abdul Hamid II also condemned the Parliament, and this resulted in a low number of Muslims participants. Despite these detractors, the 1893 World's Parliament of Religions started an international trend toward religious tolerance and interreligious dialogue which continues in the twenty-first century. There have been subsequent parliaments in 1933, 1993, 1999, 2004, 2009, and 2015. The 2015 parliament drew representatives from eighty countries and fifty different religious backgrounds.[2]

SWAMI VIVEKANANDA

Swami Vivekananda was born Narenda Nath Datta in Calcutta, India, in 1863. As the son of a lawyer, Vivekananda was able to study Western philosophy and history at both Presidency College and the Presbyterian College in Calcutta. The first major turning point in his life came when he met the famous Hindu monk Sri Ramakrishna Paramahamsa at the Dakshineshwar Kali Temple in 1881 and became his pupil. Vivekananda established a monastic order in the tradition of his teacher after Ramakrishna died in 1886. The Swami planned to live the life of a reclusive monk until his sister's suicide inspired him to venture out to learn more about his country and its people. Travelling across India in 1890 represented another major transition in Vivekananda's life. After witnessing the poverty throughout India, he decided to dedicate his life to serving the poor through charitable acts and spiritual guidance.[3]

Statue of Swami Vivekananda in India

Vivekananda saw the World's Parliament of Religions in 1893 as an opportunity to bring the teachings of Ramakrishna to the United States and secure international aid for India's impoverished. Maharajah Ajit Singh of

Khetri, India, funded the Swami's voyage to the United States. Although Vivekananda did not have a formal invitation to the Parliament, Harvard University Professor of Sanskrit John Henry Wright recommended him to the General Commission. Upon arriving in Chicago, he took up the Parliament's themes of peace, tolerance, and interreligious dialogue. Vivekananda's speech on the opening day of the conference captivated listeners and met with thunderous applause. J. H. Barrows noted the audience's appreciation for the Swami's informal manner of speaking and called Vivekananda the most influential orator of the entire seventeen days.[4]

Vivekananda introduced himself to the Parliament as a simple monk, but the sight of the Swami walking the streets of the city in his orange robe and red turban made him a celebrity among Chicagoans. Newspaper reports about his speech spread throughout the country, and his fame preceded him as he travelled across the United States over the next three years giving lectures, teaching classes, and establishing the Ramakrishna Vedanta Society in Boston, Massachusetts. Peace and interreligious dialogue were not the only issues Vivekananda spoke about during his time in the United States. He gave a lecture in Boston about the spiritual detriments of American materialism and criticized the imperialistic nature of Christian missionaries in India to an audience in Detroit, Michigan. Overall, Vivekananda saw great potential for religious tolerance in a young nation like the United States. He believed that, in contrast to his homeland of India, American culture was not permanently imprinted with an ancient religious tradition.[5]

Vivekananda's time in the United States brought him both notoriety and scrutiny back home in India. The Swami earned money for the lectures he gave while overseas and lived in the luxury of his American hosts from one city to the next. Diverging from his life as a humble monk caused him deep spiritual anguish. His consternation was exacerbated by his critics in India, who chastised Vivekananda for breaking caste. Nevertheless, after he returned to India, he founded the Ramakrishna Mission in Calcutta in 1897. The mission brought both monks and laypeople together to spread

The Ramakrishna Mission in India

the teachings of Ramakrishna and fight poverty in India. Vivekananda made a second visit to the United States from 1899 to 1900. Tragically, he died suddenly of an aneurism at the age of only thirty-nine in 1902.[6]

Swami Vivekananda's speech on the first day of the World's Parliament of Religions in 1893 remains a cornerstone of religious tolerance and interreligious dialogue in the twenty-first century. His three-year tour of the United States introduced Hindu theology and Indian culture to American society. The Swami's Ramakrishna Mission continues to provide medical aid, education, housing, disaster relief, and spiritual guidance to the needy of India.[7]

THE *BHAGAVAD GITA*

The *Bhagavad Gita* is set at a critical juncture in the epic *Mahabharata*. The *kshatriya* (warrior) Arjuna and his four Pandava brothers assemble on the battlefield across from their adversaries and cousins, the Kauravas. Though the Pandavas and Kauravas develop a bitter rivalry over inheritance, kingdom, and pride throughout the epic, Arjuna has last-minute reservations about going to war against his kinsmen. Krishna, the earthly incarnation of the god Vishnu, serves as Arjuna's charioteer and spiritual guide. Krishna addresses Arjuna's doubts and eases his mind about the dangers and tragedies of the battle ahead. Krishna's sermon to Arjuna represents the most influential text in Hindu theology across the centuries, as it outlines the basic tenets of *dharma*, *karma*, *samsara*, and *moksha*.

The *Gita* begins with Arjuna's apprehension. He questions the justification of a war that requires him to kill his own relatives, as family bonds represent one of the traditional frameworks for maintaining order in the universe. Furthermore, Arjuna sees no possibility for victory in a battle against kin, as even the winner is left to grieve the loss of loved ones. He finally pleads with Krishna to help him understand his predicament and find the proper course of action.[8]

Krishna responds by explaining *dharma* (duty). He tells Arjuna that a *kshatriya's dharma* is to fight and fight without hope for rewards or fear of loss. In fact, to not fight would be a betrayal of *dharma*, or *adharma*. *Adharma* would result in negative ramifications for Arjuna, his family, and the universe. Krishna warns Arjuna that it is "better to perform one's own work poorly than to do well the work of someone else."[9]

Krishna also explains *karma* (the positive or negative remnants of one's actions) and its effect on *samsara* (reincarnation/rebirth). He assures Arjuna that the physical body is only temporary, but that the *atman* (soul) is part of the eternal divinity present in all things. Therefore, Arjuna's sense of "self" is merely an illusion, as his true "self," or *atman*, is part of the universal divine. Each *atman* passes through many physical lives in a long cycle of rebirths before it attains *moksha* (freedom from reincarnation and oneness with the universal divine). The accumulated *karma* of one's current physical life determines the status of their next life. Krishna explains that all deeds generate either positive or negative *karma* that "will stick to them through this life and beyond, determining the nature of their rebirth."[10] In the end, Krishna convinces Arjuna to do what is best for his *karma* by following his *dharma* as a *kshatriya* and engage in battle with his enemies. Arjuna takes comfort in knowing that those who will die in the coming fight will be born again.[11]

Krishna's sermon also reveals several theological principles central to Buddhism, Jainism, and other Eastern religious traditions, such as *anicca, sunyata,* interbeing, and mindfulness. Krishna discusses *anicca* (impermanence) of physical beings when he reveals to Arjuna the temporary nature of the human body. He later engages this concept on a more abstract level when he warns Arjuna against attaching himself to the fleeting emotions of satisfaction and happiness that result from actions and accomplishments. Krishna touches upon *sunyata* (emptiness or illusory perceptions of reality) when he reveals Arjuna's deluded notion of "self." He addresses *sunyata* again when he encourages Arjuna to divorce himself from dualistic sensations and judgments of "pain and pleasure, failure and success," as these are only contrived labels for "the workings of cause and effect" that are "beyond the scope of human understanding." The "infinitely complex" mystery of the interconnectedness of all things is the tenet of interbeing.[12] Krishna alludes to interbeing when he explains to Arjuna the link between "self" and the universal divine. He later describes those who understand interbeing as seeing "themselves in all creatures and all creatures in themselves." Finally, mindfulness (ridding the mind of unnecessary distraction) is the path to acknowledging impermanence, stripping away illusions, and comprehending the complexity interbeing. When Arjuna expresses doubt about being able to clear his mind of thoughts and emotions, Krishna responds, "Without a doubt, the mind is most unruly; yet, by patient practice, by constant effort, it can be reined in under one's control." Krishna acknowledges that coming to terms with one's mortality and false sense of "self" "seems bleak initially, but as it grows it reveals itself as a precious nectar."[13]

VIVEKANANDA'S SPEECHES AT THE PARLIAMENT

Swami Vivekananda never published his own interpretation or analysis of the *Bhagavad Gita,* but he often referred to the *Gita* in his writings and speeches. Furthermore, the Swami lived his life according to the same *karma yoga* (selfless action) Krishna expressed to Arjuna in the *Gita.* Vivekananda believed all actions were either *pravritti* (actions with selfish intent) or *nivritti* (actions with selfless intent). For the Swami, *nivritti,* or *karma yoga,* meant dedicating his life to *lokasamgraha* (charitable service).[14]

Vivekananda's speeches at the World's Parliament of Religions utilized the *Gita* to advocate for religious tolerance and to illustrate the basic principles of Hinduism to an American society completely ignorant of concepts such as *dharma, karma, samsara,* and *moksha.* Vivekananda, like Ramakrishna before him, rejected dogma and religious fundamentalism.[15] He even considered ancient Hindu scripture to be fluid and open to interpretation, "by the Vedas no books are meant. They mean the accumulated treasury of spiritual laws discovered by different persons in different times."[16] The Swami believed that there are many paths to the divine for people all over the world to pursue and each person's path to the divine is their *dharma.*[17]

When Vivekananda spoke during the opening ceremony of the Parliament on 11 September 1893, he invoked the *Gita* to set the tone for interreligious dialogue and tolerance. He quoted Krishna's words to Arjuna to illustrate the multiple paths to divinity, "The present convention . . . is . . . a declaration to the world of the wonderful doctrine preached in the Gita: 'Whosoever come to Me, through whatsoever form, I reach him; all men are struggling through paths which in the end lead to Me.'"[18] In explaining India's religious tradition at the Parliament on 19 September, he described how Hinduism has historically been tolerant and inclusive of different approaches to the divine, "sect after sect arose in India" and "assimilated into the immense body of the mother faith." He described the monistic nature of religion in India as "worshippers applying all the attributes of God . . . to the images." Vivekananda proposed this Hindu/Indian approach to spirituality as a model for worldwide religious tolerance, "God is the inspirer of" temples, churches, idols, images, crosses, crescents, and books, but they "are only the supports" along the path to the universal divine which "is everywhere."[19]

Vivekananda went on to explain the key tenets of Hinduism to his audience on 19 September. He cited the *Mahabharata* to illustrate *dharma*. The Swami described how the Kauravas humiliated the Pandava brothers, stole their land, and banished them from their kingdom. Nevertheless, the Pandavas accepted their plight because they understood *dharma*. Just as Krishna enlightens Arjuna in the *Gita*, Vivekananda also explained *atman*, *karma*, and *samsara* to his American listeners that day, "I am a spirit living in a body. I am not the body . . . The present is determined by our past actions . . . The soul will go on evolving up or reverting back from birth to birth." He explained how *atman* will reach *moksha* only when it "burst" from "the bondage of matter" becomes "free from death and misery" and merges with the "universal consciousness."[20]

The 1893 World's Parliament of Religions and Swami Vivekananda represented aspirations for peace, tolerance, and charity in a world plagued by imperialistic, nationalistic, militaristic, and revolutionary dissonance. For example, while the Swami spoke out against bigotry and sectarianism in the 1890s, his home country of India was under British imperial rule. The next century would see two world wars, genocide, violent revolutions, the birth of weapons of mass destruction, and vast ideological and religious strife. Nevertheless, Vivekananda's (and Krishna's) assertion of a universal divine continues to be the spiritual foundation for worldwide efforts toward peace, religious tolerance, and human equality in the twenty-first century. The Swami's vision of a world where the "sun will shine upon . . . every human being" and there is "no place for persecution or intolerance" remains a global aspiration.[21]

QUESTIONS FOR FURTHER DISCUSSION

- Based on Swami Vivekananda's speeches in the United States, can it be said that Eastern religions, such as Hinduism, Buddhism, and Jainism, are more conducive to religious tolerance and interreligious dialogue than the Western religions of Judaism, Christianity, and Islam?

- Has the world come any closer to realizing Swami Vivekananda's aspiration for religious tolerance since 1893?

NOTES

1. "Chicago 1893: General Information," http://parliamentofreligions.org/parliament/chicago-1893; "The 1893 World's Parliament of Religions," http://www.uua.org/re/tapestry/adults/river/workshop14/178841.shtml.

2. "Chicago 1893: General Information"; "The 1893 World's Parliament of Religions"; Swami Nikhilananda, *Vivekananda: A Biography* (Calcutta, India: Advaita Ashrama, 1975), 117–18; Diana L. Eck, "Frontiers of Encounter: The Meeting of East and West in America since the 1893 World's Parliament of Religions," in *Religion and American Culture,* edited by David G. Hackett (New York: Routledge, 1995), 499.

3. "Swami Vivekananda: Life and Teachings," http://www.belurmath.org/swamivivekananda. htm; Harold W. Frank, "Swami Vivekananda's Use of the Bhagavadgita," in *Modern Indian Interpreters of the Bhagavad Gita,* edited by Robert N. Minor (New York: CUNY Press, 1986), 132.

4. "Chicago 1893: General Information"; Nikhilananda, 119, 123; Frank, 133.

5. "Swami Vivekananda: Life and Teachings"; Nikhilananda, 123, 126–27; Frank, 140.

6. "Swami Vivekananda: Life and Teachings"; Nikhilananda, 124–25, 128.

7. "Swami Vivekananda: Life and Teachings."

8. Carole Satyamurti, *Mahabharata: A Modern Retelling* (New York: W.W. Norton and Co., 2015), 402–03.

9. Ibid., 404, 412.

10. Ibid., 403.

11. Ibid., 404, 408.

12. Ibid., 405–06.

13. Ibid., 408–09, 412.

14. Frank, 131; Pavulraj Michael, "*Karma Yoga* in the *Bhagavad Gita*: Way for all to Self-Realization," *Asia Journal of Theology* (October 2014): 203–04, 209.

15. Frank, 136, 138.

16. Swami Vivekananda, *Paper on Hinduism,* http://iitk.ac.in/vs/Chicago_Speech_Of_Swami_Vivekananda.pdf.

17. Nikhilananda, 120, 122.

18. Swami Vivekananda, *Response to Welcome,* http://iitk.ac.in/vs/Chicago_Speech_Of_Swami_Vivekananda.pdf.

19. Vivekananda, *Paper on Hinduism*.

20. Ibid.

21. Ibid.

BIBLIOGRAPHY/SUGGESTED READINGS

Primary Sources

Satyamurti, Carole. *Mahabharata: A Modern Retelling.* New York: W.W. Norton and Co., 2015.

Swami Vivekananda. *Response to Welcome.* (September 11, 1893). Accessed June 20, 2016. http://iitk.ac.in/vs/Chicago_Speech_Of_Swami_Vivekananda.pdf

Swami Vivekananda. *Paper on Hinduism.* (September 19, 1893). Accessed June 20, 2016. http://iitk.ac.in/vs/Chicago_Speech_Of_Swami_Vivekananda.pdf

Monographs

Eck, Diana L. "Frontiers of Encounter: The Meeting of East and West in America since the 1893 World's Parliament of Religions." In *Religion and American Culture,* edited by David G. Hackett 495–513. New York: Routledge, 1995.

Frank, Harold W. "Swami Vivekananda's Use of the Bhagavadgita." In *Modern Indian Interpreters of the Bhagavad Gita,* edited by Robert N. Minor 131–46. New York: CUNY Press, 1986.

Swami Nikhilananda. *Vivekananda: A Biography.* Calcutta, India: Advaita Ashrama, 1975.

Articles

Michael, Pavulraj. "*Karma Yoga* in the *Bhagavad Gita*: Way for all to Self-Realization." *Asia Journal of Theology* (October 2014): 203–27.

Online Sources

"The 1893 World's Parliament of Religions." *Unitarian Universalist Association.* Accessed June 28, 2016. http://www.uua.org/re/tapestry/adults/river/workshop14/178841.shtml

"Chicago 1893: General Information." *Parliament of the World's Religions.* Accessed June 28, 2016. http://parliamentofreligions.org/parliament/chicago-1893

"Swami Vivekananda: Life and Teachings." *Ramakrishna Math and Ramakrishna Mission.* Accessed June 28, 2016. http://www.belurmath.org/swamivivekananda.htm

The Syrian Civil War: ISIS, Putin, and the International Community

Jeffrey LaMonica

> The only real way to fight international terrorism (and international terrorist groups are creating chaos in Syria and the territory of neighboring countries right now) is to take the initiative and fight and destroy the terrorists in the territory they have already captured rather than waiting for them to arrive on our soil.
>
> —Vladimir Putin, 2015

> The Assad regime bears the greatest responsibility for the 250,000 deaths of the conflict and the millions of displaced people. The systematic targeting of civilians by the regime has led to mass displacements and encouraged recruitment to and the flourishing of terrorist groups in Syria.
>
> —European Union, *Council Conclusions on Syria*, 2015

INTRODUCTION

The Assad Regime emerged in Syria with Hafez al-Assad's military coup in 1970. Bashar al-Assad succeeded Hafez in 2000 and turned his father's military dictatorship into a secular, urban, upper-class oligarchy. The Arab Spring protests against the Assad Regime erupted in 2011 and eventually escalated into a civil war.[1]

Abu Bakr al-Baghdadi founded the Islamic State in Iraq as an offshoot of al-Qaeda in 2013. Al-Baghdadi had been an active cleric and paramilitary leader in al-Qaeda since 2010. The Islamic State is comprised primarily of Sunni Wahhabists seeking to institute worldwide *sharia* law and establish al-Baghdadi as the new Sunni *caliph*. They envision this Sunni caliphate transcending the ethnic and national identities of Sunni Muslims across the globe.[2]

THE ISLAMIC STATE IN SYRIA

Islamic State forces invaded Assad's Syria in 2014. In less than a year, they controlled a strip of land from the Syrian/Iraqi border to Aleppo. Much of this occupied territory was open desert, but it did include several valuable oilfields in eastern Syria. The Syrian city of Raqqa served as the Islamic State's base of operations in Syria and the group's unofficial capital. Islamic State military forces also affected several parts of Syria outside their zone of occupation. They murdered hundreds of Kurdish civilians during their siege of Kobani, a city on the Syrian/Turkish border, from summer 2014 until January 2015. Furthermore, Islamic State forces destroyed and robbed ancient heritage sites in Palmyra in May 2015.[3]

Unlike al-Qaeda, the Islamic State is more than just a paramilitary terrorist group. It has evolved into a state-building organization with a structured military and an organized government that collects taxes, provides education, and produces propaganda. In fact, its anti-Assad propaganda has been a successful recruitment tool in Syria. The Islamic State's military forces consist of nearly thirty-one thousand paid soldiers from Syria, Tunisia, Saudi Arabia, Russia, Jordan, Morocco, France, Lebanon, Germany, Ukraine, Libya, Turkey, Pakistan, and Uzbekistan. Despite its efforts to establish itself as a sovereign nation, the international community does not recognize the Islamic State and has not engaged it in diplomatic dialogue.[4]

The Islamic State's gross domestic product was between four and eight billion dollars and its annual revenue was about five hundred million dollars in 2015. Its initial source of income came from sympathetic private donors in Saudi Arabia and Kuwait, many of whom were anxious to see the fall of the Assad Regime in Syria. Territorial conquests, however, opened new economic opportunities for the Islamic State. For example, its armed forces carried out the systematic extortion of shopkeepers and small businesses during its invasion of Syria. The Islamic State collects a 2.5 percent *zakat* from Syrian households under its occupation. One of the Five Pillars of Islam, the *zakat* is intended to be a mandatory charitable donation. The Islamic State's *zakat*, however, resembles something closer to a national income tax used for funding its government and military. Its soldiers also collect tolls from motorists travelling along roads and highways running through regions controlled by the Islamic State. Failure to comply with the Islamic State's tribute, taxation, and toll systems has resulted in vandalism and/or corporal punishment. The sale of oil became the Islamic State's largest source of revenue in 2015. It earned nearly one million dollars a day selling oil, stolen from Syrian and Iraqi oilfields, for prices far below Organization of Petroleum Exporting Countries (OPEC) rates. Smugglers moved barrels of this oil into Turkey to be sold on the black market. Finally, the Islamic State supplemented its income by ransoming hostages from Western nations and selling the antiquities pilfered Palmyra. Ransoms brought in anywhere from five to twenty million dollars per hostage in 2015.[5] The total amount of money earned through the illegal sale of artifacts remains unknown.

RUSSIAN INTERVENTION IN SYRIA

The Soviet Union formed a pact with Syria in the mid-1950s to counterbalance Turkey's inclusion in the North Atlantic Treaty Organization (NATO) by establishing a Soviet ally in the Middle East. Hafez al-Assad allowed the Soviet Union to build a naval base at Tartus on Syria's Mediterranean coast in 1971. Russian President Vladimir Putin pledged military support for the Assad Regime in September 2015. A Russian air campaign against anti-Assad forces, in conjunction with a ground operation by the Syrian Army, began in October 2015. The Russian Air Force launched about twenty airstrikes each day from airstrips in Latakia, Syria, against anti-Assad insurgents, including Islamic State forces, in Aleppo and Raqqa. The targets of these strikes included infrastructure, weapon and ammunition stores, military vehicles, and artillery positions. Meanwhile, Russian naval vessels launched cruise missiles into Syria from the Caspian Sea, nearly one thousand miles away. In November, units of the Russian Naval Infantry arrived in Syria to guard the Latakia airstrip against potential retaliatory attacks and espionage.[6]

President Putin believes the collapse of the Assad Regime and/or the partitioning of Syria will strengthen the Islamic State's position in the Middle East. Russia's strategic objectives are to remove all threats to the Assad Regime in Syria, take back all Islamic State controlled territory in Syria, rebuild war-torn Syria, and gain international recognition of Assad's government. Putin views the Russian military expedition in Syria as part of the Russian Federation's large global war on terror. The Islamic State's military forces in Syria include thousands of Russian Muslims. Putin believes it is only a matter of time until these Russian members of the Islamic State bring terrorism back home to Russia. The President told his government officials on 30 September 2015 that Russia's goal is "to take the initiative and fight and destroy the terrorists in the territory they have already captured, rather than waiting for them to arrive on our soil." According to Putin, Russia's Federal Security Service prevented twenty terrorist attacks throughout the Russian Federation between January and October 2015.[7] It is unclear how many of these abortive attacks were instigated by the Islamic State.

Putin aims to reduce the Islamic State's ability to raise money through taxes, tolls, and selling oil by driving it out of Syria. This will weaken the Islamic State's war effort by limiting its abilities to hire soldiers and purchase arms. President Putin believes long-term peace and stability in Syria can only be sustained by improving the country's infrastructure, housing, hospitals, and schools. In a speech at the Valdai International Discussion Club in Sochi, Russia, in October 2015, Putin stated, "It is clear that Syria will need massive financial, economic, and humanitarian assistance in order to heal the wounds of war."[8]

On several occasions, Putin has accused the Islamic State of twisting Islamic theology to coerce young Muslims to fight and die for its self-serving goals. He called upon legitimate Muslim leaders around the world to expose the Islamic State's deceitful religious doctrine. President Putin is confident that Bashar al-Assad is willing to comprise with all factions of Syrian society to establish a government truly representative of the

Russian Airstrikes against ISIS Forces in Kobani, Syria

people. In a meeting with Assad in November 2015, Putin said that "positive results in military operations will lay the base for then working out a long-term settlement based on a political process that involves all political forces, ethnic and religious groups." Assad concurred stating that "our common goal is to bring about the vision the Syrian people have of their own country's future."[9]

NATO'S POSITION ON SYRIA

The North Atlantic Treaty Organization is not conducting military operations in Syria as of 2015, though some of its members are a part of the United States' Coalition operating in Syria. The coalition has conducted thousands of airstrikes against the Islamic State in Syria since September 2014. The US Coalition includes the United Kingdom, Belgium, Denmark, Canada, France, and the Netherlands. NATO supports the coalition's operations against the Islamic State in Syria as part of its Global War on Terror, but condemns Russia's military intervention in Syria for contributing to turmoil and violence in the Middle East. The alliance believes that President Putin's stated objectives are only a ruse to mask his ploy to expand Russian hegemony, particularly naval presence, in the eastern Mediterranean. Chairman of the NATO Military Committee General Petr Pavel stated, "With its effort to strengthen or expand her political and military sphere of influence, Russia has become a source of regional instability."[10] NATO has also been critical of Russia's military tactics in Syria. According to NATO, the Russian Air Force's imprecise, medium-altitude, carpet-bombing sorties have caused massive collateral damage and civilian casualties in Syrian cities. Furthermore, NATO does not believe the Assad Regime will resolve conflict in Syria. NATO Secretary General Jens Stoltenberg claimed that "to support the regime is not a constructive contribution to a peaceful and lasting political solution in Syria." In fact, the organization blames the Assad Regime's chronic neglect for the needs of its people as the cause of the Arab Spring revolts in Syria in 2011 and the subsequent civil war.[11]

Finally, NATO's most pressing concern with Russia's military campaign in Syria has been safeguarding the sovereignty and integrity of Turkey, one of its member nations. Turkey claimed that Russian bombing missions in northwestern Syria in 2015 encroached upon its airspace. Jens Stoltenberg proclaimed at a press conference in October 2015, "The recent violations of Turkish airspace are unacceptable. NATO is ready to defend and protect all Allies against any threat."[12] This tension, in addition to NATO's opposition to Russia's 2014 intervention in Ukrainian affairs, has brought the relationship between NATO and the Russian Federation to an all-time low since the Cold War.

THE EU'S POSITION IN SYRIA

The European Union (EU), like NATO, is not militarily involved in Syria as of 2015. The EU is, however, conducting humanitarian efforts in Syria. The EU is also working with neighboring countries, like Turkey, Saudi Arabia, and Iran, to find a diplomatic solution for ending the Syrian Civil War and defeat the Islamic State. The EU has invited presidents Assad and Putin to participate in these conversations without success. In October 2015, EU High Representative/Vice-President Federica Mogherini stated that "we need to guarantee that political processes and transitions need to guarantee not only the safety, but also the inclusiveness of all components of societies in the process . . . Assad is and will be part of the starting point." Mogherini also acknowledged that "Russia is, and can be, a key player, when it comes to putting pressure or convincing the regime in Syria to participate in the political process." Members of the EU view Russia's indiscriminate attacks on all anti-Assad insurgents, not just Islamic State forces, as decreasing the likelihood of reaching a negotiated peace in Syria. A December 2015 EU press release stated that "Russian military attacks that go beyond the Islamic State . . . must cease immediately."[13]

PRESIDENT PUTIN'S REBUTTAL

President Putin has offered pointed responses to the objections of NATO and the EU. In regard to their critique of the Russian Air Force's methods and targets in Syria, Putin claimed that his air force accomplished more in three months than the US Coalition did in a year and a half. President Putin sarcastically invited NATO, the EU, and the US Coalition to provide the Russian Air Force with coordinates for the "correct" targets in Syria. Putin directed his own criticisms at the US Coalition's tactics in Syria. At the Valdai meeting in October 2015 he stated that "our American colleagues simply chose to airdrop weapons

Russian President Vladimir Putin

and ammunition in certain areas. I believe that this weaponry will certainly fall into the hands of terrorist organizations." He also pointed out that, unlike the US Coalition's operation in Syria, the Russian intervention was "based on the official request from the President of the Syrian Arab Republic." On the issue of the Assad Regime being removed from power in Syria, Putin claimed that "This is a matter for the Syrian people to decide."[14]

CONCLUSION

The Syrian Civil War exemplifies the complex challenges posed by ethnic, cultural, and religious diversity in nations undergoing political transition. For example, the Arab Spring revolts in 2011 appeared to be a Syrian attempt to establish a democratic form of government. Unfortunately, it degenerated into a sectarian civil war with Kurdish and Shi'ia minorities fighting against an Arab Sunni majority and the Wahhabist Islamic State.

The Syrian crisis also contrasts "universalist" with "relativist" approaches to international affairs. The "universalist" philosophy assumes there are liberal principles, such as democracy, free trade, and human rights, which all people around the world are entitled. "Relativists" asserts that each society's principles and values are dictated by its particular demographics, like ethnicity, culture, and religion. The international community employed both these philosophies in Syria in 2015. NATO, the EU, and the US Coalition were driven by their "universalist" global responsibilities to promote democracy, free trade, and human rights in their fight against the Islamic State in Syria. On the other hand, President Putin's "relativist" approach to eradicating threats to the Assad Regime was unencumbered by ideological preferences and obligations.

International interventions in Syria in 2015 exemplified a diplomatic problem many countries face when trying to balance the pursuit of their own national interests against global interconnectedness in the 21st century. Many individual countries opposed the Islamic State in Syria, but their collective efforts were limited by their own self-interests. For example, Russia, the United States, and Turkey all opposed the Islamic State in Syria, but within the parameters of their own national goals. Turkey agreed to allow the US Coalition to use their airspace to launch strikes against the Islamic State in Syria, but not Russia, its traditional enemy since the 1500s. Russia and the United States opposed each other's strategies and tactics in Syria, but both countries were wary of provoking another Cold War over this dispute. Furthermore, Russia certainly could afford an open conflict with NATO in 2015, as NATO forces outnumbered the Russian military and were well positioned in central and eastern Europe to take action against Russia if necessary. Finally, Turkey had multiple conflicting interests involving the civil war in Syria, as it opposed the Islamic State, refused to recognize the Assad Regime, and considered Kurdish Nationalism a threat to its own sovereignty. Meanwhile, the Islamic State profited from the illegal sale of smuggled oil in Turkey.[15] Russia and the international community's conflicting responses to the Islamic State's 2015 invasion of Assad's Syria exemplify the fluctuating global imbalance of power in the 21st century.

QUESTIONS FOR FURTHER DISCUSSION

- Is there any historical or theological precedence or justification for the Islamic States' goal of establishing a global caliphate?

- How, if at all, can Islamic leaders from around the world help the international community in its fight against the Islamic State?

- How does Russia's strategy in Syria compare with the United States' strategy in its Global War on Terror?

- Does the "universalist" or "relativist" philosophy represent the best approach to international affairs in the 21st century?

NOTES

1. Neil Quilliam, "Syria: The Rise of the Assads," *BBC News* (November 4, 2015). Accessed November 6, 2015. (http://www.bbc.com/news/world-middle-east-34709235)

2. "Syria Iraq: The Islamic State Militant Group," *BBC News* (August 2, 2014). Accessed November 6, 2015. (http://www.bbc.com/news/world-middle-east-24179084)

3. "Battle for Iraq and Syria in Maps," *BBC News* (November 6, 2015). Accessed November 6, 2015. (http://www.bbc.com/news/world-middle-east-27838034)

4. Ibid.; Stephen M. Walt, "ISIS as Revolutionary State: New Twist on an Old Story," *Foreign Affairs* (November/December 2015): 42, 44.

5. "Oil, Extortion, and Crime: Where ISIS Gets its Money," *NBC News* (September 11, 2015). Accessed 30 November 2015. (http://www.nbcnews.com/storyline/isis-terror/oil-extortion-crime-where-isis-gets-its-money-n200991)

6. Jonathan Marcus, "Syria Crisis: Russia's Strategy and Endgame?," *BBC News* (October 8, 2015). Accessed November 6, 2015. (http://www.bbc.com/news/world-europe-34474362)

7. Vladimir Putin, *Meeting with Officers Appointed to Senior Command Positions* (October 20, 2015). Accessed October 29, 2015. (http://en.kremlin.ru/events/president/news/50527)

8. Vladimir Putin, *Meeting of the Valdai International Discussion Club* (October 22, 2015). Accessed October 29, 2015. (http://en.kremlin.ru/events/president/news/50548).

9. Vladimir Putin, *Meeting with President of Syria Bashar Assad* (October 21, 2015). Accessed October 29, 2015. (http://en.kremlin.ru/events/president/news/50533

10. NATO, *Current Security Challenges and the Role of NATO and the European Union: Speech Delivered by the Chairman of the NATO Military Committee, General Petr Pavel, at the European Parliament* (October 20, 2015). Accessed October 29, 2015. (http://www.nato.int/cps/en/natohq/opinions_124128.htm?selectedLocale=en)

11. NATO, *Doorstep Statement by NATO Secretary General Jens Stoltenberg at the Meeting of the North Atlantic Council at the Level of Defense Ministers,* (October 8, 2015). Accessed October 29, 2015. (http://www.nato.int/cps/en/natohq/opinions_123518.htm)

12. NATO, *Press Conference by NATO Secretary General Jens Stoltenberg following the Meeting of the North Atlantic Council in Defense Ministers Session* (October 8, 2015). Accessed October 29, 2015. (http://www.nato.int/cps/en/natohq/opinions_123522.htm)

13. European Union, *Doorstep Remarks by High Representative/Vice-President Federica Mogherini ahead of the Weekly European Commission College Meeting* (October 14, 2015). Accessed October 29, 2015. (http://eeas.europa.eu/statementseeas/2015/151014_01_en.htm); European Union, *Remarks by High Representative/Vice-President Federica Mogherini at the Press Conference after the Foreign Affairs Council* (October 12, 2015). Accessed October 29, 2015. (http://eeas.europa.eu/statements-eeas/2015/151012_05_en.htm); European Union, *Council Conclusions on Syria* (October 12, 2015). Accessed October 29, 2015. (http://www.consilium.europa.eu/en/press/press-releases/2015/10/12-fac-conclusions-syria/)

14. Vladimir Putin, *Meeting with Government Members* (September 30, 2015). Accessed October 29, 2015. (http://en.kremlin.ru/events/president/news/50401); Putin, *Meeting of the Valdai International Discussion Club.*

15. "Oil, Extortion, and Crime: Where ISIS Gets its Money."

BIBLIOGRAPHY/SUGGESTED READINGS

Primary Documents

European Union. *Doorstep Remarks by High Representative/Vice-President Federica Mogherini ahead of the Weekly European Commission College Meeting.* (October 14, 2015). Accessed October 29, 2015. http://eeas.europa.eu/statementseeas/2015/151014_01_en.htm

European Union. *Remarks by High Representative/Vice-President Federica Mogherini at the Press Conference after the Foreign Affairs Council.* (October 12, 2015). Accessed October 29, 2015. http://eeas.europa.eu/statements-eeas/2015/151012_05_en.htm

European Union. *Council Conclusions on Syria.* (October 12, 2015). Accessed October 29, 2015. http://www.consilium.europa.eu/en/press/press-releases/2015/10/12-fac-conclusions-syria/

NATO. *Current Security Challenges and the Role of NATO and the European Union: Speech Delivered by the Chairman of the NATO Military Committee, General Petr Pavel, at the European Parliament.* (October 20, 2015). Accessed October 29, 2015. http://www.nato.int/cps/en/natohq/opinions_124128.htm?selectedLocale=en

NATO. *Press Conference by NATO Secretary General Jens Stoltenberg following the Meeting of the North Atlantic Council in Defense Ministers Session.* (October 8, 2015). Accessed October 29, 2015. http://www.nato.int/cps/en/natohq/opinions_123522.htm

NATO. *Doorstep Statement by NATO Secretary General Jens Stoltenberg at the Meeting of the North Atlantic Council at the Level of Defense Ministers.* (October 8, 2015). Accessed October 29, 2015. http://www.nato.int/cps/en/natohq/opinions_123518.htm

Putin, Vladimir. *Meeting of the Valdai International Discussion Club.* (October 22, 2015). Accessed October 29, 2015. http://en.kremlin.ru/events/president/news/50548

Putin, Vladimir. *Meeting with President of Syria Bashar Assad.* (October 21, 2015). Accessed October 29, 2015. http://en.kremlin.ru/events/president/news/50533

Putin, Vladimir. *Meeting with Officers Appointed to Senior Command Positions.* (October 20, 2015). Accessed October 29, 2015. http://en.kremlin.ru/events/president/news/50527

Putin, Vladimir. *Meeting with Government Members.* (September 30, 2015). Accessed October 29, 2015. http://en.kremlin.ru/events/president/news/50401

Monographs

Bell, Daniel A. *Beyond Liberal Democracy: Political Thinking for an East Asian Context*. Princeton, NJ: Princeton University Press, 2006.

Nye, Jr., Joseph S. *Is the American Century Over?*. Malden, MA: Polity Press, 2015.

Weber, Steven and Bruce W. Jentleson. *The End of Arrogance: America in the Global Competition of Ideas*. Cambridge, MA: Harvard University Press, 2010.

Articles

"Battle for Iraq and Syria in Maps." *BBC News* (November 6, 2015). Accessed November 6, 2015. http://www.bbc.com/news/world-middle-east-27838034

Marcus, Jonathan. "Syria Crisis: Russia's Strategy and Endgame?" *BBC News* (October 8, 2015). Accessed November 6, 2015. http://www.bbc.com/news/world-europe-34474362

"Oil, Extortion, and Crime: Where ISIS Gets its Money." *NBC News* (September 11, 2015). Accessed November 30, 2015. http://www.nbcnews.com/storyline/isis-terror/oil-extortion-crime-where-isis-gets-its-money-n200991

Quilliam, Neil. "Syria: The Rise of the Assads." *BBC News* (November 4, 2015). Accessed November 6, 2015. http://www.bbc.com/news/world-middle-east-34709235

"Syria Iraq: The Islamic State Militant Group." *BBC News* (August 2, 2014). Accessed November 6, 2015. http://www.bbc.com/news/world-middle-east-24179084

Walt, Stephen M. "ISIS as Revolutionary State: New Twist on an Old Story." *Foreign Affairs* (November/December 2015): 42–51.

CHAPTER V

The Universality of Human Rights

Race, Rights, and Slave Culture

Joseph Myers

One day, when all our people were gone out to their works as usual, and only I and my dear sister were left to mind the house, two men and a woman got over our walls, and in a moment seized us both, and, without giving us time to cry out, or make resistance, they stopped our mouths, and ran off with us into the nearest wood. . . . I therefore determined to seize the first opportunity of making my escape, and to shape my course for that quarter; for I was quite oppressed and weighed down by grief after my mother and friends; and my love of liberty, ever great, was strengthened by the mortifying circumstance of not daring to eat with the free-born children, although I was mostly their companion. While I was projecting my escape, one day an unlucky event happened, which quite disconcerted my plan, and put an end to my hopes. I used to be sometimes employed in assisting an elderly woman slave to cook and take care of the poultry; and one morning, while I was feeding some chickens, I happened to toss a small pebble at one of them, which hit it on the middle and directly killed it. The old slave, having soon after missed the chicken, inquired after it; and on my relating the accident (for I told her the truth, because my mother would never suffer me to tell a lie) she flew into a violent passion, threatened that I should suffer for it; and, my master being out, she immediately went and told her mistress what I had done. This alarmed me very much, and I expected an instant flogging, which to me was uncommonly dreadful; for I had seldom been beaten at home. I therefore resolved to fly; and accordingly I ran into a thicket that was hard by, and hid myself in the bushes. Soon afterwards my mistress and the slave returned, and, not seeing me, they searched all the house, but not finding me, and I not making answer when they called to me, they thought I had run away, and the whole neighbourhood was raised in the pursuit of me. In that part of the country (as in ours) the houses and villages were skirted with woods, or shrubberies, and the bushes were so thick that a man could readily conceal himself in them, so as to elude the strictest search. The neighbours continued the whole day looking for me, and several times many of them came within a few yards of the place where I lay hid. I then gave myself up for lost entirely, and expected every moment, when I heard a rustling among the trees, to be found out, and punished by my master: but they never discovered me, though they were often so near that I even heard their conjectures as they were looking about for me; and I now learned from them, that any attempt to return home would be hopeless.

—Gustavus Vassa, *The Interesting Narrative of the Life of Olaudah Equiano*, 1789

Olaudah Equiano was a slave who became free, and his writings about what slaves endured revolutionized the world. Throughout his life Olaudah Equiano was known by his slave name of Gustavus Vassa and in 1789 he published an autobiography, *The Interesting Narrative of the Life of Olaudah Equiano*. Equiano's writings were widely read in the English speaking world in which Equiano had been enslaved and then lived as a free African. Equiano, according to his account, was enslaved in his native Nigerian village and then transported into the Caribbean as a teenager around 1757. By his early 20s Equiano had been sold to owners in the British colonies of North America, where he was finally able to purchase his freedom from an owner that was a

The Caribbean Slave Trade in the 1700s

© Everett Historical/Shutterstock.com

Quaker in 1766. The Quakers were beginning to advocate the end of slavery as an institution. Slavery had been around in some form for thousands of years and had not been challenged. Equiano's writings, and then his activism, brought exposure to the horrors of slavery, and historians attribute his efforts as instrumental in the passage of Britain's *Slave Trade Act* of 1807, which outlawed the slave trade out of West Africa.

It is more than likely that no slave throughout history, whether in Ancient Rome or in Virginia in 1832, wanted to be a slave. But the idea of slavery as an illegitimate concept that is morally unacceptable is a new idea—new meaning only within the last few hundred years. Most cultures throughout time accepted the idea that some people are born to rule and that some are born to serve. In those cultures even slaves accepted the idea that slavery was just part of human society. Perhaps they dreamed of being free, but they did not dream of a day where no one was a slave. In western Europe in the post-Renaissance Enlightenment world philosophers, at first, and then activists, began to think that all human life could be or should be what individuals wanted to make of their own life. These visionaries believed that a person's position at birth should not determine their whole life. By the mid 18th century the political belief that men should be able to determine their own lives was becoming more popular in the British world. In America that this new idea found a home, though at first it was only thought to apply to men of European descent, but the idea of self-definition and self-determination would form the basis for application to other people regardless of race or gender. The idea has taken time to realize. The first great hurdle applied to slavery. The ability for people to see all humans as individuals necessitated a change in values. Even in America most people still believed in the 18th and 19th century that birth (your race, your gender, your orientation) determined what rights you should have. And to change a value system the cultural psychology had to change. Writings like those of Equiano helped bring about that change.

Cape Coast Slave Fort in Ghana

© nicolasdecorte/Shutterstock.com

The following passage presents a chance to read an account of slavery from the slave's perspective. Equiano's writing makes it clear that Atlantic World slavery was a system that was more than just the enforced labor of Africans. The evidence that Equiano develops displays the physical brutality inflicted on the enslaved, but perhaps even more important Equiano's vivid accounts relates the cultural psychology that was being formed because of slavery. Understanding cultural psychology within a historical context is not easy. You have to interpret evidence, which is usually physical action, in light of the psychological consequences those actions have. The patterns that emerge from those consequences then reveal the possibility of the cultural psychology that is formed. That cultural psychology will then in turn further inform other actions and the feelings based on those actions. What that means is that actions create psychological responses—feelings, attitudes, perceptions. Accumulated feelings, attitudes and perceptions of an environment, even those formed through the physical or geographic environment, entails the cultural psychology of that environment. The cultural psychology of the Atlantic Slave trade, therefore, effected not only the Africans who were slaves, but Europeans as well. The Slave Trade and Slavery in the New World had a profound psychological environment, which manifested as white supremacy and black dehumanization is one which still affects us today.

QUESTIONS FOR FURTHER DISCUSSION

- In what ways does Equiano personalize the slave experience so that his readers understand that slaves were individuals? In what ways does Equiano show that the violence against the slaves also dehumanized and diminished the individual being of Europeans?

- How does Equiano show that a cultural psychology based on violence is destructive? How does that destructivity differ from those inflicting violence and those upon which violence is inflicted?

- Do you think current racial attitudes that see less value in black lives could have developed through white violence on black people in slavery?

Aux Armes
The Declaration of the Rights of Man and the Citizen in Global Perspective

Anthony Makowski

> Freedom of Speech . . . just watch what you say.
>
> —Ice-T, *Freedom of Speech*, 1989

> The struggle of man against power is the struggle of memory versus forgetting.
>
> —Milan Kundera, *The Book of Laughter and Forgetting*, 1978

The debate over both the differences and needs for positive human rights (those rights that a government should not only confer but promote) versus negative human rights (inalienable rights that should not be abridged by a modern government) remains constant, and often heated, in modern society. With the desire to be sympathetic to the social and cultural traditions of a diverse community, the attempts to create a truly universal basket of human rights for over seven billion on the planet remains, to put it mildly, illusive. In the study of modern civilization, one consistent theme concerns the role of individual rights and the attempts to expand human rights to a greater number of individuals.

There are many instances, both rebellious and revolutionary, that one could consider when attempting to understand the expansion of modern liberties. One time period often under consideration is that of the late eighteenth century. Here, the age of the "Atlantic Revolutions" sought to fundamentally challenge established orders of government and found new societies based on reason and, in the abstract, equality. One of these revolutions, the French Revolution, would serve as a good example of how the unleashing of revolutionary ideas (much like a genie out of a bottle) would lead to acts that would both enthrall and frighten much of the world.

The French Revolution is perhaps best seen as the French Revolution**s**. From 1789–1799, if one wishes to exclude the years of the Napoleonic Revolution, France would move from an attempt to create a constitutional monarchy to the establishment of a full, monarchy purged, republic. While the call for enlightened rule had been gaining strength in France among the middle and, to some degree, upper classes for many years, more recent events in the 1780s would push France toward first revolt and then revolution.

When we think of revolution, or at least the unrest or violence that accompanies a revolution, we often need a villain or scapegoat. As is often the case in determining causation in history (What did what and when . . .), trying to find a true villain that sums up all the problems facing France in the late eighteenth century is difficult to do. One can start at the top of the political food chain and consider the rule, and eventual fate, of Louis XVI (perhaps soon to be deemed, with the help of the guillotine, Louis the Short).

One of the more basic problems for Louis XVI would be that his office, the monarchy, reflected too well the contradictions and corruption within the French government by the eighteenth century. Louis himself was intrigued by the ideas of the Enlightenment which sought to correct errors and place greater faith in science and reason to better the lives on the individual. As an example, Louis himself was a locksmith of modest skill—he viewed gadgets and inventions with a keen sense of interest. However, the new

The Execution of Marie Antoinette in 1793

inventions that could bolster the rule of the monarch could also help to spur ideas that would crack the foundations of monarchy. Lost wars, a system of taxation that called on peasants and the middle class to give up as much as half of their yearly income, often meager, to their lords or the state, bad harvests, and bad press (if that was not enough there were others) would conspire to help doom the French monarchy in the eyes of many. A consistent rule of history is that when force can no longer compel the obedience of subjects, force can later be used to topple seemingly old and outdated systems of government. For revolutions the need to place blame on one individual as a representation of the rot within politics and society is often critical. Unfortunately for Louis, and his wife Marie-Antoinette, they were by time, circumstance and temper tailor-made for this role.

The summer of 1789 in Paris, like many a summer in Paris, was hot. In a last attempt to try and resolve a crisis of government finance, Louis XVI had decided to call representatives from France, drawn from the clergy, nobility, middle class, and peasantry, to try and break the financial crisis and secure new sources of revenue for the crown. At first, many in the Estates General, as the body that would deliberate over the financial crisis would be known, felt that the crown was trying to legitimately solve a state crisis. For members of the Third Estate (the middle class and the peasantry) the meeting of the Estates General was seen as an opportunity to make the tax code both more efficient and fair. Ultimately, through some missteps by Louis, a failure to read the signs of potential rebellion by the First (Clergy) and Second (Nobility) Estates, and a series of almost laughable circumstances, the Third Estate became disillusioned with the process and began to refer to themselves by another name—The National Assembly.

The endgame for many a government is when it loses control of the capital city. Few cities are more capital in global history than Paris. As concern grew that the monarchy, in alliance with the First and Second Estates would ultimately disband and disperse, or worse, the Third Estate many sought to find ways to defend themselves and their interests. This defense would, as often happens in sports, eventually turn to offense.

Many tourists who travel to Paris wish to see certain sights—the Eiffel Tower, the Louvre, the twenty or so Starbucks that can be found within four or five blocks of each other. One place that still commands some interest is the Bastille. However, while it commands interest it does not command a physical location in Paris today. The Bastille, a hated symbol of absolutism with a less than happy history, was ultimately destroyed during the French Revolution (one set of keys was given to the Liberator-Hero of the United States—George Washington). National Independence Day for France remains July 14. It was on this date in 1789 that the Third Estate, with some help from an enthusiastic crowd, stormed the Bastille, overwhelmed the garrison, and learned its strength. In our contemporary world we often see, or perhaps participate in, the contrasting calls of the need for restraint and order versus those who demand action now (protests for civil rights, protests for civil rights to be protected). For France, the moment when absolutism ended both physically and symbolically, was July 14, 1789.

Revolts often follow the pattern of lather, rinse, and repeat. Most are in response to unsustainable physical and psychological conditions that force individuals to push back against the perceived oppressor (or the agents of the oppressor). For the French Revolution, which can be thought of as beginning with the storming of the Bastille, the quandary was what to do with this new strength and, more directly, what new type of

Storming the Bastille on 14 July 1789

government would better reflect the needs of French citizens. Only a few, at this stage, wished to eliminate the monarchy entirely. It had, after all, been a ruling part of French society for many centuries and had served as a symbol, at least in the good times, of cohesion. The next debate would concern how to begin the process of modernizing French society. Opening a formerly "closed" system of government is dangerous business indeed. If one moves too fast then an individual can soon find themselves out of power, or worse, in a manner similar to the government that was just overthrown. If one moves too slow then the momentum is lost, and the old regime may regain control.

The National Constituent Assembly, as it now called itself, had begun to draft what was to be a preamble for a new French constitution (France would have several constitutions come and go during the French Revolution and in later years). Many of the drafters of this preamble sought to create a document that would be based on the Enlightenment principles of reason and practicality. To put together a true set of rights for citizens was, and remains, a daunting task. How far does one go? Does one include all individuals? What types of property restrictions are there on citizenship? There is a reason why law codes are both very common and consistent throughout global history, but declarations of human rights codified by states are a more recent development. The resulting document produced by the National Constituent Assembly would be known as *The Declaration of the Rights of Man and the Citizen*. The final article of this document would be passed on August 26, 1789.

1. Men are born and remain free and equal in rights. Social distinctions may be founded only upon the general good.
2. The aim of all political association is the preservation of the natural and imprescriptible rights of man. These rights are liberty, property, security, and resistance to oppression.

3. The principle of all sovereignty resides essentially in the nation. No body nor individual may exercise any authority which does not proceed directly from the nation.

4. Liberty consists in the freedom to do everything which injures no one else; hence the exercise of the natural rights of each man has no limits except those which assure to the other members of the society the enjoyment of the same rights. These limits can only be determined by law.

5. Law can only prohibit such actions as are hurtful to society. Nothing may be prevented which is not forbidden by law, and no one may be forced to do anything not provided for by law.

6. Law is the expression of the general will. Every citizen has a right to participate personally, or through his representative, in its foundation. It must be the same for all, whether it protects or punishes. All citizens, being equal in the eyes of the law, are equally eligible to all dignities and to all public positions and occupations, according to their abilities, and without distinction except that of their virtues and talents.

7. No person shall be accused, arrested, or imprisoned except in the cases and according to the forms prescribed by law. Any one soliciting, transmitting, executing, or causing to be executed, any arbitrary order, shall be punished. But any citizen summoned or arrested in virtue of the law shall submit without delay, as resistance constitutes an offense.

8. The law shall provide for such punishments only as are strictly and obviously necessary, and no one shall suffer punishment except it be legally inflicted in virtue of a law passed and promulgated before the commission of the offense.

9. As all persons are held innocent until they shall have been declared guilty, if arrest shall be deemed indispensable, all harshness not essential to the securing of the prisoner's person shall be severely repressed by law.

10. No one shall be disquieted on account of his opinions, including his religious views, provided their manifestation does not disturb the public order established by law.

11. The free communication of ideas and opinions is one of the most precious of the rights of man. Every citizen may, accordingly, speak, write, and print with freedom, but shall be responsible for such abuses of this freedom as shall be defined by law.

12. The security of the rights of man and of the citizen requires public military forces. These forces are, therefore, established for the good of all and not for the personal advantage of those to whom they shall be entrusted.

13. A common contribution is essential for the maintenance of the public forces and for the cost of administration. This should be equitably distributed among all the citizens in proportion to their means.

14. All the citizens have a right to decide, either personally or by their representatives, as to the necessity of the public contribution; to grant this freely; to know to what uses it is put; and to fix the proportion, the mode of assessment and of collection and the duration of the taxes.

15. Society has the right to require of every public agent an account of his administration.

16. A society in which the observance of the law is not assured, nor the separation of powers defined, has no constitution at all.

17. Since property is an inviolable and sacred right, no one shall be deprived thereof except where public necessity, legally determined, shall clearly demand it, and then only on condition that the owner shall have been previously and equitably indemnified.

The later periods of the French Revolution would put many of the ideas, and hopes, contained in this document to an extreme test. Indeed, in the next five years France would move from revolution to radical revolution to counter-revolution. Many of the French governments that claimed to uphold the values of *The Declaration of the Rights of Man and the Citizen* would, in many respects, trample on those rights (particularly Articles VIII and IX). The period of the Reign of Terror in 1793 and 1794 would unleash a river of blood throughout Paris and the French countryside as the new revolutionary government sought to defeat both internal and external enemies. With the outbreak of war with Austria and Prussia in 1792, the stakes of the revolution became even higher. Many of the monarchs in Europe could almost feel an invisible blade at their necks that threatened their rule. If it happened in France, it could happen anywhere. Later, a young general who won both quick and lucrative victories on the battlefield, Napoleon Bonaparte, would harness the ideals of the French Revolution to help him both preserve and destroy the ideals seen in 1789.

In the two centuries since the final defeat of Napoleon, the debate continues over the source of individual rights. Are rights conferred by birth or are they conferred, and guarded, by the state? Is it possible to truly draft a singular document that addresses the natural and civil rights of each citizen? What does this say about other cultures and nations who take different views, often more collective, on civil rights and the needs of society?

QUESTIONS FOR FURTHER DISCUSSION

- The first two articles of the *Declaration of the Rights of Man and the Citizen* offer sweeping statements regarding the natural rights of man. What do you think is meant by "common benefit" in Article I? What natural rights are outlined in Article II? How could one interpret "security and resistance from oppression"?

- In the opening discussion of this chapter a distinction was made between "positive" human rights and "negative" human rights. Provide examples where the Declaration of the Rights of Man and the Citizen promotes both positive and negative human rights.

- Review Article XVI. Does this article seem to imply that only certain countries offer a true protection of rights to their citizens?

The British Second Empire 1830–1914

James Esposito

We find that your country is distant from us about sixty or seventy thousand miles, that your foreign ships come hither striving the one with the other for our trade, and for the simple reason of their strong desire to reap a profit. Now, out of the wealth of our Inner Land, if we take a part to bestow upon foreigners from afar, it follows, that the immense wealth which the said foreigners amass, ought properly speaking to be portion of our own native Chinese people. By what principle of reason then, should these foreigners send in return a poisonous drug, which involves in destruction those very natives of China? Without meaning to say that the foreigners harbor such destructive intentions in their hearts, we yet positively assert that from their inordinate thirst after gain, they are perfectly careless about the injuries they inflict upon us! And such being the case, we should like to ask what has become of that conscience which heaven has implanted in the breasts of all men?"

—Lin Zexu's Letter to Queen Victoria, 1839

Take up the White Man's burden—
Send forth the best ye breed—
Go bind your sons to exile
To serve your captives' need;
To wait in heavy harness,
On fluttered folk and wild—
Your new-caught, sullen peoples,
Half-devil and half-child.

> Take up the White Man's burden—
> In patience to abide,
> To veil the threat of terror
> And check the show of pride;
> By open speech and simple,
> An hundred times made plain
> To seek another's profit,
> And work another's gain.
>
> —Rudyard Kipling, *The White Man's Burden*, 1899

INTRODUCTION

The British Empire had lost the American colonies in the late eighteenth century, but grew more secure and powerful in the wake of the Battle of Waterloo. With Napoleon defeated and France momentarily contained, Britain became the preeminent imperial power at the beginning of the Victorian era. Loss of America had been a severe blow, but Britain's overall presence in India and China grew. The East India Company ruled the Indian subcontinent as monopoly business, a privatized economic engine and was key to Britain's trade strategy in the Far East. Britain's new factories churned out cheap textiles for Indian market, but there were few goods to trade with China.

The Daoguang Emperor's trade restrictions were challenged many times by European trade missions. Several, including Britain's Macartney Mission of 1793, became notable confrontations between European commercial interests and Chinese state. By the early Victorian period restrictions upon trade became increasingly intolerable for British traders and politicians alike. Free trade if in theory, if not in practice, was a top priority for a generation of British leaders like Lord Palmerston who demanded to access Asian markets for their manufactured goods.

AN EMPIRE OF TRADE, 1830–1880

Naval power built the British Empire. The valuable commodities like sugar and tea made money for the state through taxes and excise during the eighteenth century.[1] These taxes allowed the state to build more and better fighting ships to protect trade from North America to the Far East. The large number of armed conflicts (Seven Years War, American Revolution, and Napoleonic War) helped build Britain's navy into the strongest in the world.[2]

Tea quickly became one of the largest and most important commodities for Britain. The British public imported large amounts of tea (now essential consumption for all social classes), porcelain, and other Chinese products. China was the only source of supply in the early nineteenth century. Housed in one of the few trading

"Factories"(merchant houses) in Canton, the British traded silver for tea. The British traded away much of their silver to China, and without any goods to sell, they faced huge trade deficits.[3] British merchants had limited access to the Chinese market even if buyers for British goods could be found.

Opium was the solution. Opium was produced in India and highly sought after in China. While used in India and Great Britain itself, the drug's popularity in China grew exponentially leading up to the First Opium War in 1839. The East India Company contracted dealers in China's interior from its Factory in Canton and reached large sections of the population. The opium trade, taxed and paid to the British government, helped pay for imperial expansion. Britain could not have paid for its expanding military and colonial presence without the opium trade.[4] Trade in opium turned the net loss of silver to a huge gain, weakening China's economy and hurting state revenue.

The British government was well aware of the deleterious effects of the drug. Opium had caused large selections of Chinese society to fall into addiction and illness, but its sale continued under the economic justification of free trade.[5] By the 1840s, opium amounted to over 10% of all Indian revenue. By the end of nineteenth century, the opium trade would be valued in the tens of millions of pounds per year.[6] The silver bullion earned from the opium trade made its way back to British banks, strengthening the pound and freeing money for other investments throughout the nineteenth century. This capital was essential for transition from a commercial-capitalist economy to industrial-capitalist one.

Lin Zexu's letter to Queen Victoria illustrates just how destructive the opium trade was to Chinese society. Zexu had been selected by the Emperor to crack down on the trade in the drug, but discovered that it would be impossible to rid the country of opium without targeting the traders who imported it. Commissioner Zexu was angry that while China exported useful and socially beneficial goods like tea and porcelain, the Chinese received opium in return. He implied that the opium trade may have been a deliberately hostile act designed to undermine the imperial throne and sicken the Chinese people. He took a hard line approach on the opium trade and organized the destruction of British opium stores outside Canton and imprisoned a large number of Chinese merchants and intermediaries.

Palmerston interpreted Lin Zexu's anti-opium policy as an aggressive act which falsely imprisoned British subjects and wantonly destroyed property. The government declared war in March of 1839. Over the following three years the British would defeat the Chinese decisively in a series of sea and land battles at Canton (1841), Chapu (1842), and Chianking (1842).[7] The British military defeated numerically superior Chinese forces through skillful use of new technologies such as rifles and early steamships as well as impressive military leadership of General Hugh Gough, a veteran of the Napoleonic Wars.[8] The First Opium War ended in the Treaty of Nanjing and inaugurated the era of gunboat diplomacy.

The Treaty of Nanjing opened up a series of Treaty Ports, or coastal cities under European control. Four coastal cities would be allowed to trade with the Europeans without restrictions, including the ports of Canton and Shanghai. The treaty also required the Chinese government to pay an enmity to British merchants as well as take formal responsibility for the conflict. Great Britain received the colony of Hong Kong. The treaty set up a pattern of military and political defeat at the hands of Europeans,

Battle of Chapu, 1842

United States, and Japanese. Chinese historians have called this era of turmoil the "Century of Humiliation."[9] China became a marginalized, semi-colony from the 1842 until the Communist Revolution in 1949. Hong Kong was not returned to Chinese authority until 1997.

China's trade restrictions became a symbol of perceived Asian arrogance and disrespect to Westerners. Many saw China as oriental despotism, unchanging and oppressive bureaucracy that valued tradition above all else.[10] Europeans, British in particular, saw themselves as distinctly different, dynamic, and industrious people compared to the Chinese. Ascribing any attribute to an entire nation is wrong, but it nevertheless provided a discursive basis for the Opium War. The confrontation over opium foregrounded the attributes the British wanted to see within themselves, justifying their actions when the conflict was about restricting the trade in harmful drugs.

THE WHITE MAN'S BURDEN, NEW IMPERIALISM, 1880–1914

British imperialism changed and evolved over time. By the 1880s, imperialism took on a distinctly new phase. Exploration of Africa by British explorers like Livingstone and Burton made clear that the continent was "backward" and required European intervention. Europeans employed anthropological knowledge to identify and find out the nature of tribal societies, particularly in southern Africa. Anthropological and geographical exhibitions, often supported by Royal Anthropological Institute and Anthropological Society of London, looked toward Africa as a great test of European will and ingenuity. Unlike China or the Middle East, Africa was seen as the bottom of the developmental ladder.

For British missionaries and explorers, Africa was truly a challenge. The tribal societies of southern Africa had animist religious practices, but no civilization that was legible to European society. Instead of highlighting a shared human experience or exploring African history at greater depth, explorers brought attention to cultural and religious differences of native peoples focusing on how they were different, strange, and inferior. Captured African people were often exhibited in colonial exhibitions in London, Paris, and elsewhere. The anthropological value of Africa was a useful anchor for the imperial project. It allowed Europeans, the British in particular, to understand themselves better. Africa gave a fixed position in which to compare their own society. For the British, they always defined themselves as free rather than unfree, industrious rather than slothful, inventive instead of traditional, and modern rather than unmodern. Of course none of these traits can be ascribed to an entire nation, but it rather justified the violence of imperial project, provided a sense of purpose, and mission for their actions.

David Livingstone

The British had originally thought African differences were caused by tropical environment. They believed that climate determined national virtues and that hotter climates were invariably prone to negative traits like sloth, inefficiency, and inferior intellectual capacity.[11] Alternatively, the reason that Europeans had developed relatively rapidly and made large commercial and military empires was that they had a natural climate edge. The cool climate of Western Europe made the best of all possible peoples; hot and humid climates less so. By the 1880s, climate determinism had declined as a prominent scientific theory. The formal science of race, borrowing elements from Charles Darwin, Herbert Spencer, and Francis Galton, argued that there was a hierarchy of racial types.[12] However, these types were not dictated by climate, but rather fixed sub races of the same species. It was thought Europeans, again, were endowed with the most desirable attributes. Asians and Native Americans less so. Africans, due to their low perceived level of development, were confined to the very bottom of the evolutionary ladder.

Africans became the childlike object of the imperial project. Britain and the other European powers believed they had a unique duty, the White Man's Burden. Kipling's poem illustrates just how seriously these ideas were taken. Kipling wrote the poem during the Spanish-American war, a late colonial conflict, was a kind of initiation for the United States. The British had been involved with the new imperialism for some time, and Kipling formally spelled out the odious duty for Europeans (and the United States) to go forth and improve, by force if necessary, the backward peoples of the world. Europe would bring modernity coupled with its own embedded ideas of what made a virtuous citizen, family, and society. Africans were never asked if they wanted this dubious 'honor' and those who resisted were often injured or killed by European armies.

Technological development also made access to the African continent possible in ways it had not been previously. Steamers, telegraph, and modern prophylaxis against tropical diseases like malaria made organized occupation of the region possible.[13] The machine gun also played a role in African conflicts—its efficient design and firepower decimated native armies and kept the population under control with a minimal number of troops.[14] Artillery and self-loading rifles only added to the impressive technological advantages of European armies in Africa. European scientific and technological superiority also reinforced embedded ideas of white superiority. Not only would European paternalism guide African social and cultural development, it also belittled their use of tools and toolmaking to improve society.[15]

The New Imperialism had its own economic and political dimension. Britain, Germany, and the other major powers had industrialized by the late nineteenth century. With their home markets exhausted, all the colonial powers looked towards their empires for new markets and new opportunities for economic growth. The industrialists and politicians focused on integrating new African colonies into the modern capitalist world economy. Increasingly British colonies became less of a place to buy and more as a market to sell to.[16] The imperial project opened a large number of new material requirements and expectations for society. African colonies gradually moved from subsistence agriculture to commodity production, producing tea, coffee, and other commodities for sale on the world market.[17]

European powers also looked toward their colonies for mineral wealth.[18] South Africa had probably the largest deposits of precious metals and diamonds in the world, and the British government moved quickly to capture the Boer states in 1902. Economic development became one of the major justifications for the imperial project. Just as European anthropological knowledge marked Africa as racially inferior, it also implied that they had an inferior claim to the resources of the region. Europeans were best placed to encourage the material development of Africa and its integration into the world market. This paternalism influenced all aspects of the colonizer–colonized relationship.

European competition increasingly marked African imperialism. Britain, France, and Germany as well as Belgium and Italy jockeyed for position at international conferences. The Berlin Conference of 1884 formally craved up much of the continent up to the European powers.[19] Each nation wanted to secure as much land area as possible. From the British perspective, African colonies were essential for the new strategic imperative of the steam-powered naval ships. In order to maintain Britain's naval superiority, it would need many coaling stations on the coast of Africa. Coaling stations themselves became hubs of trade and commerce, as well as railheads for access to the African interior.

CONCLUSION

The era of 1830–1914 might be best described as two British empires. The empire of trade starting with the events leading up to the First Opium War until 1880 marked the transition from commercial-capitalism to industrial-capitalism. Chinese restrictions on trade became intolerable and Britain used military force to open up China in a very early instance of "gunboat diplomacy." 1880 to the beginning of the First World War might be best described as the beginning of a formal imperial project, where scientific and anthropological knowledge was marshalled to justify occupation and transformation of life in Africa under European control. In both cases empire was an essential mirror to help the British try to understand who they were as a people and who they imagined themselves to be.

QUESTIONS FOR FURTHER DISCUSSION

- What led to the First Opium War? How did the tea trade effect British policy in China?

- How and why did the British Navy become the preeminent naval power? How did taxes on goods like tea and later opium pay for it?

- Compare Lin Zexu and Kipling's pieces. How did the discourses of empire change from 1840 to 1899? What anchored empire in the Zexu's day? How was that different than Kipling's era?

- How did anthropological and scientific knowledge change European understanding of Africa? What role did race play in the New Imperialism?

NOTES

1. John Brewer, *The Sinews of Power: War, Money, and the English State, 1688–1783* (London: Routledge, 1994), 21–35.

2. Brewer, *Sinews of Power*, 156–160.

3. Carl A. Trocki, *Opium Empire and Global Political Economy: A Study of the Asian Opium Trade 1750–1950* (New York: Taylor & Francis, 1999), 42–43.

4. Trocki, *Opium Empire and Global Political Economy*, 9.

5. Peter Ward Fay, *The Opium War, 1840–1842: Barbarians in the Celestial Empire in the Early Part of the Nineteenth Century and the War by Which They Forced Her Gates Ajar* (New York: University of North Carolina Press, 1998), 72.

6. John F. Richards, "The Opium Industry in British India," *The Indian Economic and Social History Review* 39, nos. 2 and 3 (2002): 149–178.

7. Fay, *The Opium War*, 261–332.

8. Fay, *The Opium War*, 289–300.

9. David Scott, *China and the International System, 1840–1949: Power, Presence, and Perceptions of a Century of Humiliation* (Albany: SUNY Press, 2008), 8–23.

10. An extensive look at orientalism is outside the scope of this chapter. Edward Said's *Orientalism* (1978) explores European notions of the orient at greater length.

11. Catherine Hall, *Civilising Subjects: Metropole and Colony in the English Imagination 1830–1867* (Chicago: University of Chicago Press, 2002), 48–49.

12. Daniel J. Kevles, *In the Name of Eugenics: Genetics and the Uses of Human Heredity* (Cambridge, MA: Harvard University Press, 1995), 70–75.

13. Daniel R. Headrick, *The Tools of Empire: Technology and European Imperialism in the Nineteenth Century* (New York: Oxford University Press, 1981), 58–78.

14. Headrick, *Tools of Empire*, 116–118.

15. Michael Adas, *Machines as the Measure of Men: Science, Technology, and Ideologies of Western Dominance* (Baltimore: Cornell University Press, 1992), 153–166.

16. Eric Hobsbawm, *The Age of Empire: 1875-1914* (London: Vintage Books, 1989), 66–68.

17. Hobsbawm, *The Age of Empire*, 60–65.

18. Thomas Pakenham, *The Scramble for Africa, 1876–1912* (New York: Random House, 1991), 375.

19. Pakenham, *The Scramble for Africa*, 250–255.

BIBLIOGRAPHY/SUGGESTED READINGS

Hall, Catherine. *Civilising Subjects: Metropole and Colony in the English Imagination 1830–1867*. Chicago: University of Chicago Press, 2002.

Headrick, Daniel R. *The Tools of Empire: Technology and European Imperialism in the Nineteenth Century*. New York: Oxford University Press, 1981.

Hobsbawm, Eric. *The Age of Empire: 1875–1914*. London: Vintage Books, 1989.

Pakenham, Thomas. *The Scramble for Africa, 1876–1912*. New York: Random House, 1991.

Trocki, Carl A. *Opium Empire and Global Political Economy: A Study of the Asian Opium Trade 1750–1950*. New York: Taylor & Francis, 1999.

CHAPTER VI

Global Peacekeeping

Four Days in November

Jeffrey LaMonica

Surrender in good condition by the German armies of the following war material: Five thousand guns (2,500 heavy, and 2,500 field), 25,000 machine guns, 3,000 *minenwerfer*, 1,700 airplanes (fighters, bombers—firstly, all of the D 7'S and all the night bombing machines). . . . Evacuation by all German forces operating in East Africa within a period to be fixed by the Allies. . . . The following financial conditions are required: Reparation for damage done. While such armistice lasts no public securities shall be removed by the enemy which can serve as a pledge to the Allies for the recovery or reparation for war losses. . . . German surface warships which shall be designated by the Allies and the United States shall be immediately disarmed and thereafter interned in neutral ports or in default of them in allied ports to be designated by the Allies and the United States.

—*Armistice*, 1918

Delegates from Imperial Germany met with Supreme Allied Commander Marshal Ferdinand Foch in the French forest of Compiegne on 8 November 1918 to accept the terms of a ceasefire that would end the Great War. The German envoys requested hostilities cease immediately while they communicated the details of the armistice to Berlin and waited for their government to grant them permission to sign the agreement. Foch rejected this appeal and insisted that military operations continue until after the Germans signed the document. This was the moment of revenge Marshal Foch and his staff had been waiting for since 1871, when the Imperial German Army defeated the French in the Franco-Prussian War and stripped them of the territories of Alsace and Lorraine. Foch's decision to keep military pressure on the Germans until the armistice was signed prolonged the conflict until 11 November. Needless to say, these additional four days proved especially costly for soldiers fighting on the western front.

German Delegates Meet with Marshal Ferdinand Foch on 8 November 1918

Marshal Foch first displayed a determination to secure a non-negotiable armistice with Germany well before the meeting at Compiegne on 8 November. The Allied Supreme War Council met in Paris to draft an armistice proposal on 26 October 1918. At the conference, French President Raymond Poincare warned against making the armistice conditions so demanding as to cause Germany to reject them and continue fighting into 1919. Foch's response to Poincare illustrated his willingness to beat the Imperial Germany into complete submission, "Then we will continue the war . . . until they (Allied armies) have . . . seized guarantees fully ensuring peace—a peace we will have obtained at the price of unestimable sacrifices!"[1] At the same meeting, American diplomat Edward "Colonel" House asked Foch if he preferred an immediate armistice. Foch replied, "I am not waging war for the sake of waging war. If I obtain through the armistice the conditions that we wish . . . I am satisfied. Once this objective is attained, nobody has the right to shed one drop more of blood."[2] Nevertheless, this sentiment was not consistent with Foch's demeanor nine days later at Compiegne.

The Allied Supreme War Council finalized their armistice terms on 4 November and authorized Marshal Foch to meet with representatives of the Imperial German Government. The next day, President of the United States Woodrow Wilson sent a message to Berlin offering an armistice calling for a fair, equitable peace settlement based on his Fourteen Points. The Germans then assembled their own armistice commission. Their motorcar convoy left German Supreme Headquarters in Spa, Belgium, at midnight on 7 November with orders to negotiate the best terms possible for Germany, but also to bring an immediate end to the war. German Chancellor Max von Baden told the commission's head delegate Secretary of State Matthias Erzberger to "Obtain what mercy you can, Matthias, but for God's sake, make peace."[3] Secretary Erzberger would soon discover that his Allied counterpart was adamantly opposed to the former and indifferent concerning the latter.

At 12:30 a.m. on 7 November, Marshal Foch received a telegram from German Supreme Headquarters informing him that their armistice commission was on its way. The message requested that "in the interest of humanity, the arrival of the German delegation . . . might cause a provisional suspension of hostilities."[4] Foch responded by designating a safe location where the envoys could pass through the French lines, but ignored the German plea for an immediate ceasefire. Foch then left his headquarters for Compiegne by train at 5 p.m.[5]

After encountering fog, rain, muddy road conditions, and a motorcar accident, the German armistice commission finally arrived at Compiegne at 7 a.m. on 8 November. The initial meeting between Marshal Foch and the German delegates took place two hours later in the dining car of Foch's train. Prior to the German's arrival, Foch exclaimed to his staff that "We'll be polite, but we must show them who we are."[6]

Secretary Erzberger and his plenipotentiaries presented Marshal Foch with their credentials baring Chancellor Baden's signature and granting them "full power" to conduct negotiations in the name of the Imperial German Government. Foch acted intentionally aloof and inquired into the purpose of their visit. Erzberger stated that they had come to receive the Allied armistice proposal. Foch then claimed he had "no proposal to make" and "no conditions to give." Needless to say, an uncomfortable silence followed. Erzberger began to read aloud President Wilson's message from 5 November.[7] Foch interrupted Erzberger and insisted he ask formally to be presented with the armistice. Foch's peculiar behavior was meant to insinuate that the Allied armistice terms were not negotiable.[8]

The process of reading and translating all the components of the armistice took two hours. The first section called for the "Cessation of hostilities by land and in the air six hours after the signing of the Armistice."[9] The next part dealt with the surrender of weapons and vehicles, the Imperial German Army's evacuation of the Rhineland, and the repatriation of Allied prisoners of war. Another condition demanded the German withdrawal from Russia and Africa. A financial section called for the "Reparation for damage done." Naval stipulations outlined the surrender of all German warships and declared that the British Navy's blockade of Germany would continue even after the armistice went into effect.[10] The armistice's terms concerning Germany's disarmament, loss of territory in Europe and Africa, and monetary retribution would reappear as critical clauses in the 1919 Treaty of Versailles.

After the terms were read, Secretary Erzberger requested an immediate cessation of hostilities. Marshal Foch refused, "it is impossible to stop military operations until the German delegation has accepted and signed the conditions which are the very consequence of those operations."[11] The German delegation then presented Foch with a note from German Supreme Headquarters, "During this time, the struggle between our armies will continue and will inevitably take toll of numerous victims, among the troops and the people, who will have fallen needlessly at the last minute and who might be preserved for their families."[12] This plea did nothing to change Foch's mind.

The meeting adjourned at 11:30 a.m. Marshal Foch permitted his German guests to use his wireless telegraph to inform Chancellor Baden in Berlin that a courier was leaving for German Supreme Headquarters with a draft of the armistice. The message noted that "an immediate agreement to suspend hostilities provisionally was rejected by Marshal Foch."[13] In Paris, French Prime Minister Georges Clemenceau wept when he learned that the armistice negotiations were progressing. He exclaimed, "I saw 1870 again, the defeat, the shame, the loss of Alsace-Lorraine, and now all that is wiped out."[14]

For the rest of the day on 8 November, the German delegates expressed their concerns about the armistice terms. They objected to the continuation of the British naval blockade, claiming it would create a famine in Germany. They also protested the surrender of machine guns and artillery, stating this would make it impossible for the Imperial German Army to quell the antiwar riots and political rebellions that had already erupted in the German cities of Hamburg, Altona, Lubeck, Wilhelmshafen, Brunsbuttel, and Cuxhaven. Furthermore, just as President Poincare had predicted, the German plenipotentiaries accused the Allies of intentionally making the armistice conditions harsh to force the war into 1919 and cause the total collapse of Imperial Germany. At the end of the day, Marshal Foch invited the German envoys to put their grievances in writing.[15]

Secretary Erzberger and the German commission presented Marshal Foch with their written *Observations on the Conditions of an Armistice with Germany* on 9 November. Foch responded to the German grievances the next day with his *Answer to the Observations on the Conditions of an Armistice with Germany*. His note insisted that no questions concerning the armistice terms could be entertained until the envoys received a reply from Chancellor Baden in Berlin. Meanwhile, Kaiser Wilhelm II's abdication of the German throne resulted in Friedrich Ebert replacing Baden as chancellor on 10 November. This shift of power, however, had no impact on Erzberger and the commission's authority to sign the armistice. Erzberger received a transmission from Berlin at 7 p.m. on 10 November granting him permission to sign the armistice.[16] The commission received an additional confirmation from Chief of the German General Staff Field Marshal Paul von Hindenburg. Hindenburg's telegram, however, urged Erzberger to make one last effort to amend the armistice conditions and suggested military operations end the moment the document was signed.[17]

Secretary Erzberger and the German commission finally met with Marshal Foch to sign the armistice at 2:15 a.m. on 11 November. Following General Hindenburg's request, the German delegates spent three hours making one final attempt to negotiate more favorable terms. Foch agreed to reduce the number of machine guns to be surrendered and extended the deadline for the German Army's evacuation of occupied territories from fourteen to fifteen days. Erzberger tried to protest the continuation of the naval blockade, but Foch took the opportunity to remind the German envoys of the hardships suffered by France and Britain as a result of Germany's unrestricted submarine campaign against Allied shipping.[18]

Marshal Foch and his staff signed the armistice at 5:10 a.m. on 11 November 1918. Secretary Erzberger and the other German envoys signed as well, but expressed their reservations about the settlement in writing, "the carrying out of this agreement may plunge the German people into anarchy and famine." One of Foch's officers cabled the news of the armistice to the front at 5:40 a.m., and the official ceasefire went into effect at 11 a.m.[19]

© Everett Historical/Shutterstock.com

American Troops Celebrating the Armistice on 11 November 1918

Nothing occurred militarily between 8 and 11 November to bring the Imperial German Army any closer to total defeat on the western front. Allied forces were not able to drive the Germans out of France and Belgium, invade Germany, or force large contingents of German soldiers to surrender during those four days. Marshal Foch's decision to prolong the war only served to increase the already horrific casualty figures of the Great War. British Army Captain B. H. Liddell Hart's postwar memoirs criticized Foch's choice, "Realizing that his Armistice terms would give him all the fruits of victory, he sacrificed the ornamental laurels which might, or might not, have come from a continuation of the fight, at the price of more lives."[20]

QUESTIONS FOR FURTHER DISCUSSION

- What were the benefits, if any, of Marshal Ferdinand Foch extending the Great War by four days? Was this decision made entirely out of France's thirst for revenge against Imperial Germany?

- In which ways did the terms of the armistice set the stage for the Treaty of Versailles? How would this shape European affairs in the 1920s and 1930s?

NOTES

1. Ferdinand Foch, *The Memoirs of Marshal Foch*, trans. Colonel T. Bentley Mott (Garden City, NY: Doubleday, Doran, and Company, Inc., 1931), 461.
2. Ibid., 463.

3. Stanley Weintraub, *A Stillness Heard Round the World: The End of the Great War: November 1918* (New York: Truman Talley Books, 1985), 46; Rod Paschall, *The Defeat of Imperial Germany 1917–1918* (Chapel Hill, NC: Algonquin Books, 1989), 223; Harry R. Rudin, *Armistice 1918* (Archon Books, 1967), 320.

4. Foch, 466.

5. Ibid.; Rudin, 336.

6. B. H. Liddell Hart, *Foch: the Man of Orleans* (Boston: Little, Brown, and Co., 1932), 400.

7. Rudin, 322.

8. Liddell Hart, 401; Alan Palmer, *Victory 1918* (New York: Atlantic Monthly Press, 1998), 280.

9. Foch, 478.

10. Ibid., 482, 484.

11. Ibid., 470.

12. Liddell Hart, 402.

13. Foch, 472.

14. Rudin, 342.

15. Foch, 473.

16. Ibid., 475; Rudin, 370.

17. Rudin, 379; Francis Whiting Halsey, *The Literary Digest History of the World War: Compiled from Original and Contemporary Sources: American, British, French, German, and Others, Volume VI* (New York: Funk and Wagnalls, 1920), 241.

18. Liddell Hart, 404.

19. Foch, 487.

20. B. H. Liddell Hart, *Reputations: Ten Years After* (Boston: Little, Brown, and Co., 1928), 175.

BIBLIOGRAPHY/SUGGESTED READINGS

Foch, Ferdinand. *The Memoirs of Marshal Foch*. Translated by Colonel T. Bentley Mott. Garden City, NY: Doubleday, Doran, and Company, Inc., 1931.

Halsey, Francis Whiting. *The Literary Digest History of the World War: Compiled from Original and Contemporary Sources: American, British, French, German, and Others, Volume VI*. New York: Funk and Wagnalls, 1920.

Liddell Hart, B. H. *Reputations: Ten Years After*. Boston: Little, Brown, and Co., 1928.

---. *Foch: The Man of Orleans*. Boston: Little, Brown, and Co., 1932.

Palmer, Alan. *Victory 1918*. New York: Atlantic Monthly Press, 1998.

Paschall, Rod. *The Defeat of Imperial Germany 1917–1918*. Chapel Hill, NC: Algonquin Books, 1989.

Rudin, Harry R. *Armistice 1918*. Archon Books, 1967.

Weintraub, Stanley. *A Stillness Heard Round the World: The End of the Great War: November 1918*. New York: Truman Talley Books, 1985.

The Evolution of American Interventionism

Kevin Cahill

It is not true that the United States feels any land hunger or entertains any projects as regards the other nations of the Western Hemisphere save such as are for their welfare. All that this country desires is to see the neighboring countries stable, orderly, and prosperous. Any country whose people conduct themselves well can count upon our hearty friendship. If a nation shows that it knows how to act with reasonable efficiency and decency in social and political matters, if it keeps order and pays its obligations, it need fear no interference from the United States. Chronic wrongdoing, or an impotence which results in a general loosening of the ties of civilized society, may in America, as elsewhere, ultimately require intervention by some civilized nation, and in the Western Hemisphere the adherence of the United States to the Monroe Doctrine may force the United States, however reluctantly, in flagrant cases of such wrongdoing or impotence, to the exercise of an international police power.

—Theodore Roosevelt, *Fourth Annual Message*, 1904

We have made clear that the war on terror is an ideological struggle between tyranny and freedom. When President Truman spoke here for the 150th anniversary of West Point, he told the class of 1952, "We can't have lasting peace unless we work actively and vigorously to bring about conditions of freedom and justice in the world." That same principle continues to guide us in today's war on terror. Our strategy to protect America is based on a clear premise: The security of our

Nation depends on the advance of liberty in other nations. On September the 11th, 2001, we saw that problems originating in a failed and oppressive state 7,000 miles away could bring murder and destruction to our country. And we learned an important lesson: Decades of excusing and accommodating the lack of freedom in the Middle East did nothing to make us safe. So long as the Middle East remains a place where freedom does not flourish, it will remain a place where terrorists foment resentment and threaten American security.

—George W. Bush, *West Point Commencement Address*, 2006

INTRODUCTION

This article focuses on two documents: Theodore Roosevelt's 1904 annual message, which introduced the Roosevelt Corollary to the Monroe Doctrine, and George W. Bush's commencement address at West Point in June of 2002, which was one of a collection of speeches that outlined his Bush Doctrine. In these speeches, Roosevelt and Bush established two fundamental changes in American foreign policy. This essay examines the events that prompted them and outlines the changes that they conveyed.

THE ROOSEVELT COROLLARY

In his 1904 State of the Union Address, Roosevelt announced his addendum to the Monroe Doctrine. His revision introduced a more assertive foreign policy in the Western Hemisphere but, it was a natural progression from the changes that began in the preceding decade. Beginning in 1823, the Monroe Doctrine was one of the keystones of American foreign policy. At the time, the Monroe Administration became alarmed at reports of a Spanish design to regain control over its former colonies. To deter Spain and other European efforts to establish new colonies in the Western Hemisphere, the United States promised not to interfere in the existing European colonies in the Western Hemisphere but would resist any effort to establish future European colonies. In this way, the Monroe Doctrine was a defensive mechanism designed to contain European influence in the Region. However, by the 1890s, the first signs of a more confident and aggressive agenda became apparent when Richard Onley, Grover Cleveland's Secretary of State, announced that the Western Hemisphere was the United States' sphere of Influence.

Onley's comments illustrated the emergence of a more forceful foreign policy that was best illustrated in the Spanish-American War in 1898. The successful conclusion of the War enabled the US to annex Guam, the Philippines, and Puerto Rico. The Spanish American War also demonstrated the fact the United States foreign policy in the Hemisphere was changing from a defensive mindset to an offensive mindset. It showed a growing sense of confidence that would enable the US to initiate efforts

President Teddy Roosevelt

to expel outside powers from the region. The removal of the Spanish from Cuba and Puerto Rico at the conclusion of the Spanish-American war demonstrated the success of this new policy.[1]

The Spanish-American War showed the United State's growing power in the region, but US dominance was far from secured. Throughout the 1890s, European nations were increasing their influence in the area. In 1895, the British Navy seized the Nicaraguan port of Corinto to force that country to address property damages and intervened in a boundary dispute between Venezuela and British Guiana. The later incidence, which became known as the First Venezuelan Crisis caused tensions to escalate between the United States and Great Britain, which briefly led to a talk of war. Of greater importance, the French were intensifying their efforts to complete the construction of a canal across the Panamanian Isthmus.[2]

On September 6, 1901, Leon Czolgosz, a Polish anarchist, unwittingly sparked a series of events that would beget one of the key events in the Western Hemisphere: the United States' gaining control over the Panama Canal. Czolgosz's assassination of William McKinley thrust Theodore Roosevelt into the White House at a critical juncture in American history. The nation had defeated Spain, secured control over the Philippines, Guam, and Puerto Rico; and was primed to secure its dominance in the region. The new President was determined to seize the opportunity and help transform the United States into one of the Great Powers.[3]

Two problems interfered with Roosevelt's ambitions. The first was a deficiency of the Monroe Doctrine. As historian Serge Ricard notes, "Yet Monroe's 'doctrine' showed a glaring inadequacy: nowhere was the U.S. preeminence among the American Republics clearly stated." Ultimately, Roosevelt would revise the Monroe Doctrine to assert the United States' right to secure hegemony in Latin America.[4]

The second obstacle to American supremacy was European investment in Latin America and the subsequent chaos and conflict that followed. Once debt began to accumulate, European investors pressured their government to use their military to coerce repayment. European countries had already intervened in Egypt, Turkey, Serbia, and Greece, and American government officials feared similar actions would follow in the Western Hemisphere. Roosevelt also concluded that the Monroe Doctrine exacerbated the problem by inferring it protected Latin American debtor nations from the coercive efforts used by European nations to recoup their debt.[5]

Roosevelt's first words on the subject of Latin American debt indicates that he initially accepted the status quo in the region, and would act only to resist any further European territorial ambitions. He agreed that European governments had the right to protect the financial and business interests of their nationals in Latin America. In his first State of the Union address in 1901, he said, "we do not guarantee any state against punishment if it misconducts itself, provided that punishment does not take the form of the acquisition of territory of any non-American power." He would later add that "if any South American country misbehaves toward any European country, let the European country spank it." The Venezuelan crisis of 1902–1903 would force him to rethink this policy.[6]

The roots of the Second Venezuelan Crisis stretched back to the preceding decade when European nationals invested heavily in the Venezuelan economy. Germans had significant financial interest in manufacturing and agriculture, Belgians owned the majority of the nation's water facilities, and French investors controlled Venezuela's cable communications. At the same time, Venezuela was engulfed in a civil war with the victor, Castro, securing the presidency in 1899. Upon becoming president, Castro faced a grave financial crisis that resulted from the pressure applied by the European government's demand for repayment for the property destroyed during the two years of civil war. Additionally, Germany and Great Britain demanded redress for the non-payment of interest on a $10 million dollar Venezuelan bond.[7]

The crisis began at the end of November 1902, when Cipriano Castro ignored the British and German ultimatum that required immediate repayment. Initially, Roosevelt failed to issue any protests toward the European demand, as it was a typical behavior of great powers. When German Ambassador Theodore Von Holleben informed the State Department of the blockade, Secretary of State John Hay replied that the blockade was justified and the United States would not intervene as long as Germany and Great Britain respected the sovereignty of Venezuela. However, the United States became concerned when the German gunboat *Panther* shelled the Venezuelan customs house in San Carlos on January 17, 1903, and sank several Venezuelan warships. Roosevelt sent an ultimatum to the German government demanding that they allow the US to intervene. After that, Germany and Britain agreed to allow the International Court at the Hague to arbitrate the dispute.[8]

Despite Roosevelt's support for arbitration, many historians conclude that the President became concerned after the ruling was announced, and drafted the Roosevelt Corollary to avoid the consequence that would result from it. The terms, which the Hague announced in 1904, stipulated that the settlements involving Great Britain, Italy, and Germany would be given preference. Although Venezuela was in debt to many foreign nations, the Hague ruled that it must repay Britain, Germany, and Italy before paying the other creditor. The Hague Court concluded that Germany, Italy, and Great Britain deserved preference because they had financed the military operations that forced Venezuela to agree to arbitration. From the United States' vantage point, the Hague ruling indicated that military intervention was the most effective method of securing repayment. Roosevelt believed that the decision would encourage European nations to send troops into the Western Hemisphere, which would undermine the United States' ambitions to secure hegemony over the region.[9]

To prevent these kinds of situations from arising, Roosevelt announced his Corollary to the Monroe Doctrine. In it, he inferred that the United States would assume the role of a regional police force with authority to maintain law and order. He insisted that the United States had the right to intervene and settle disputes involving Latin American nations and their European creditors. As long as the United States fulfilled this role, this solution to the Latin American debt problem would ease the concerns of the European creditors, and they would stop pressuring their governments to intervene. After that, US officials made numerous public announcements that ensured the nation was committed to upholding the Roosevelt Corollary. Roosevelt also sent the Great White Fleet on a global tour to demonstrate the United States had the means to enforce the Roosevelt Corollary. US commitment to upholding the Doctrine was established in 1905 when the United States prevented Italy from ordering military forces into the Dominican Republic to secure payment on a defaulted bond. American gunboats and Marines arrived in Santo Domingo, the nation's capital, and took over the collection of customs duties and sent forty-five percent of the money collected to pay off foreign creditors.[10]

Economics also played a role in the development of the Monroe Doctrine. First, as Secretary of War Elihu Root noted, Latin America was a critical market for America. In the period between 1897 and 1908, American foreign investment rose from 0.7 billion 2.5 billion, and roughly half of this went to Latin America. Latin America was also an important market for manufactured goods. As historian Walter LaFeber notes in his book, *The New Empire: An Interpretation of American Expansion 1860–1898*, American policy makers were overly concerned with the unstable economic development that accompanied the rapid rise in industrialization in the post-Civil War Period. In 1893, the United States experienced the worst depression in history, and many assumed that one of the primary problems was the inability of domestic markets to keep pace with manufacturing. LaFeber argues that securing foreign markets, especially in nearby Latin America, seemed a logical solution to the problem.[11]

Another reason for securing hegemony over the Western Hemisphere was the American plan to build the Panama Canal. France began the effort to build a canal across the Panamanian isthmus, but they were unable to surmount the numerous obstacles and make much progress. Despite the difficulties of the French, the United States was keenly interested in building the canal. Many prominent men from President McKinley to Alfred Mahan, believed that the successful construction of a canal was vital to United States' economic and military potential. Initially, McKinley opted for the Nicaraguan route, but upon becoming president, Theodore Roosevelt chose Panama. However, after the Columbian Congress rejected the agreed-upon Treaty, Roosevelt became furious and told Elihu Root, "I do not think the Bogota lots of jackrabbits should be allowed permanently to bar one of the future highways of civilization." Roosevelt responded by supporting the Panamanian rebels and ordered the USS Nashville to prevent Columbia from suppressing the subsequent rebellion. The Hay-Bunau-Varilla Treaty signed on 18 November 1903, provided the United States a grant of land 10 miles wide in which the United States was virtually sovereign. The United States would pay $10 million and after nine years pay an annual fee of $250,000.[12]

Roosevelt drafted his addendum to the Monroe Doctrine to prevent the arrival of European troops and gunboats in Latin American Ports. Keeping the hemisphere free from European forces was not novel, but demanding the right to intervene in the internal affairs of sovereign nations was new and demonstrated a dramatic change in the American diplomacy. Before 1910, Roosevelt and then his successor Robert Taft sent American troops into Cuba, Haiti, Nicaragua, and Panama. In many ways, Roosevelt's "Big Stick" diplomatic style was continued and became the foundation for the US foreign policy in Latin America for the 20th century.[13]

THE BUSH DOCTRINE

Almost 100 years after Roosevelt introduced the Roosevelt Corollary, George W. Bush and his neoconservative advisors Donald Rumsfeld, Dick Cheney, and Paul Wolfowitz launched the Bush Doctrine, which also marked a significant departure from past policies. The President and his advisors announced their expansion of American foreign policy objectives in NSS 2002 and a series of speeches, one of which was Bush's commencement address at West Point on 1 June 2002. Bush identifies four main tenets that became the foundation of the Bush Doctrine.

The four tenets of the Bush Doctrine include the right to wage preemptive wars, the right to act unilaterally, the need to maintain military supremacy and dominance, and the necessity of spreading freedom, democracy, and free enterprise. George W. Bush

US Army Helicopters in Baghdad

and his advisors recognized that the period after the September 11 attacks provided an excellent opportunity to extend American influence and eliminate threats to American security and global stability.[14]

Understanding the events that occurred in the decade before its implementation is vital to understanding the rationale for the Bush Doctrine. In 1991, the collapse of the Soviet Union and the end of the Cold War made many American policymakers believe the United States' victory in the Cold War demonstrated the superiority of the American way of life. It further cemented their belief in American exceptionalism, which is the idea that the United States is embodied with unique values that include: liberty, egalitarianism, individualism, and laissez-faire. All of these values made the US uniquely qualified to lead the world. They firmly believed that the principles of liberal democracy were global, and all humanity aspired to live in a democratic country. They also echoed Woodrow Wilson's faith in the peacemaking aspects democracy; democracies did not go to war against one another, and thus the spread of democracy would promote peace and stability throughout the world. Lastly, they believed that promoting democracy would also benefit the United States by making the world safer and more open to American commerce.[15]

These beliefs would be tested in the First Gulf War when Saddam Hussein invaded Kuwait in August of 1990. Within a month, the United Nations responded by levying economic sanctions and establishing an embargo on Iraq. After these measures had failed to force Iraq to withdraw from Kuwait, the UN authorized a military response. Concurrently, the George H. W. Bush administration formed a coalition against Iraq, which was announced on 10 January 1991. Six days later the First Gulf War began. Within two days of the deployment of ground forces, the Coalition routed the Iraq Army and Hussein quickly ordered his troops to withdraw from Kuwait.

The decimation of the Iraqi forces created a debate within the Bush Administration. One faction was led by Secretary of Defense Dick Cheney and Cheney's top advisor Paul Wolfowitz. They argued that it was a mistake to end the conflict before the Coalition removed from Hussein from power. They explained that if he remained in power, Iraq would continue to be a threat to the United States and our Allies in the region. Because the United States had encouraged Shia militants in southern Iraq to rebel, the United States was responsible to protect them from government reprisals. Wolfowitz and Cheney were disappointed when the United States failed to step in and prevent the death of thousands of militants. Colin Powell, who was then Head of the Joint Chiefs of Staff, and National Security Advisor Brent Scowcroft commanded a rival faction. They argued that the Coalition Forces had fulfilled the UN mandate and evicted Iraq from Kuwait and did not have the authority to remove Hussein. They also were concerned about becoming entangled in the civil war after the Coalition Forces removed Hussein.[16]

Much to the dismay of Cheney and Wolfowitz, the President ultimately agreed with Powel and Scowcroft and decided to end the ground assault and allow Hussein to remain in power. This decision elicited three key results. First, Hussein had to be contained and to achieve this the UN retained the economic sanctions on Iraq until 1997. While the sanctions failed to have a significant impact on the Iraqi dictator, they created a humanitarian crisis in Iraq, which led to the death of approximately one million Iraqi civilians. In addition to the economic sanctions, the Iraqi government was required to allow UN weapons inspectors to have complete access to any weapons facilities in Iraq to ensure it was refraining from developing any nuclear, biological, and chemical weapons. The Iraqi government's efforts to thwart the ability of the weapons inspectors was a continued source of contention between Iraq, the United Nations, and the United States.[17]

Another outcome[18] of the survival of the Hussein government was the creation of the Wolfowitz Doctrine, which became the blueprint for the Bush Doctrine. Dismayed by the limited nature of the victory in the Gulf War, Wolfowitz wrote a policy paper that he hoped would be the foundation for the nation's defense policy for the next decade. In the draft of the Defense Planning Guide Wolfowitz wrote,

> Our first objective is to prevent the re-emergence of a new rival, either on the territory of the former Soviet Union or elsewhere, that poses a threat on the order of that posed formerly by the Soviet Union. This is a dominant consideration underlying the new regional defense strategy and requires that we endeavor to prevent any hostile power from dominating a region whose resources would, under consolidated control, be sufficient to generate global power. These regions include Western Europe, East Asia, the territory of the former Soviet Union, and Southwest Asia.

Wolfowitz's recommendations are similar to many of the tenants that later appeared in the Bush Doctrine. In general, his draft identified the end of the Cold War as an opportunity and a challenge for the United States to take the necessary steps to maintain a global hegemony.[19]

Astounded and alarmed by the aggressive nature of his recommendations, some of Wolfowitz' colleagues at the Pentagon leaked a draft to *The New York Times*.[20] However, the uproar that followed caused Bush to order Cheney to write a new draft that eliminated the sections calling for preemptive strikes and unilateralism and instead retain the nation's commitment to containment and multilateralism. Nonetheless, Wolfowitz's ideas would be resurrected in the fall of 2001.

Before the September 11th attacks, George Bush shared his father's view of the Wolfowitz Doctrine. While campaigning for the presidency, his speeches indicated a deep skepticism for the expansive foreign policy espoused by the Neoconservatives. Furthermore, he also criticized the Clinton Administration's efforts to promote nation building as naive and overreaching. Bush promised that his foreign policy would be much narrower in focus and target more realistic goals. Until the September 11 attacks, his principal advisors were Colin Powell and National Security Adviser Condoleezza Rice, who shared his cynicism of unilateral and hegemonic policies that were embraced by the Neoconservatives. Although neoconservatives like Vice President Dick Cheney, Secretary of Defense Donald Rumsfeld, and Assistant Secretary of Defense Paul Wolfowitz occupied prominent positions in the Bush government, Bush largely ignored their recommendations.[21]

The September 11 attacks caused Bush to immediately change his focus from adhering to the Realists' policy objective of his father, Powell, and Scowcroft, to embracing the neoconservative objectives of establishing American global dominance and spreading democracy. This change in focus would lead to the implementation of the Bush

Doctrine, the invasion of Iraq in 2004, and ultimately the rise of the Islamic State of Iraq and Syria (ISIS) and the general instability in the Middle East.

One of the first tenets that Bush and his new allies hoped to implement was the spread of free enterprise and democracy throughout the world and particularly in the Middle East. The September 11 Attacks created the environment which would make this possible. The loss of close to three thousand Americans lives and the fear and anger that followed it ensured that the Administration would have the support necessary to implement the policies that appeared preposterous only a decade before. The Administration believed that freeing Iraq from the severe constraints of the Hussein Regime and assisting Iraq in building a stable democracy would be the most effective method of spreading democracy throughout the Middle East. They firmly believed in the universal appeal of democracy and saw no issues of incompatibility between Islam and American culture. They assumed spreading democracy in the Middle East would enhance American security, and promote stability and peace in the region while eroding the appeal of terrorist groups. They also expected that the eventual globalization of this policy would benefit all mankind; toppling oppressive governments that habitually violated international agreements, intimidated and tormented their neighboring countries, and repressed their citizens. After the September 11 attacks, Bush informed his closest advisers that, "we have an opportunity to restructure the world toward freedom, we have to get it right." At a news conference in March of 2002, he informed the White House Press Corp that, "We understand history has called us into action, and we are not going to miss that opportunity to make the world more peaceful and more free."[22]

Despite this hopeful view, the Neoconservatives had a pessimistic perception of the current global environment. For the Bush administration, the Al-Qaida attacks demonstrated that the world was a dangerous place and would become more dangerous if the United States failed to take the initiative against the rogue states that harbored terrorist organizations and stockpiled weapons of mass destruction. The administration concluded that the failure to rectify this situation increased the likelihood of a devastating attack on the United States and its allies. Consequently, they assumed that the containment policy and brinkmanship of the Cold War would not succeed in deterring these groups from attacking the United States. They understood the nation's military might alone would not successfully prevent terrorists from initiating first strikes because they were non-state actors,[23] which significantly increased the difficulty of launching successful retaliatory attacks. As a result, they feared that Al-Qaida and other militant terrorist organizations would strive to secure weapons of mass destruction and use them against the United States.[24]

The architects of the Bush Doctrine stressed the imminent nature of the threats against the United States. Given the destructive power of nuclear, biological, and chemical weapons, and the recognition that terrorist groups were willing to accept the risks associated with first strikes, it was vital to stop the growth of terrorist organizations before they could secure these weapons and organize plots to use them. Condoleezza Rice informed CNN on September 8, 2002, that it was too risky to wait for conclusive evidence to emerge, "we don't want the smoking gun to become a mushroom cloud."[25]

The Bush Administration assumed that terrorist organizations were fanatics who would do anything to achieve their goals. This assumption led them to conclude that the only way to thwart terrorist attacks was to initiate preemptive wars against nations that harbored terrorists and shared in their plan to destroy Western civilization. The Bush Administration quickly identified the new "Axis of Evil," which included: North Korea, Iran, and Iraq. The repressive and violent actions and policies of these countries combined with their ceaseless effort to develop weapons of mass destruction, their known ties to terrorist groups, and their staunch anti-American rhetoric provided the sufficient evidence to demonstrate their intentions to harm the United States. Although in many ways North Korea was a greater threat, the United States would focus on Iraq.

The Bush Doctrine is also based on the presumption that only the United States possessed the power and resolve to combat the dangers presented by rogue nations and terrorist groups. This assumption caused them to reject the more cooperative foreign policy dictates of traditional American policy and adopt unilateralism. It was no longer safe to hinge our actions on the ability of diplomats to secure the support of our allies. The Bush Doctrine rejected the multilateral approach that had been a key component of American foreign policy since World War II.

Taking a leadership role in world affairs has been the responsibility of the nation since World War II. However, until the Bush Doctrine, the United States made sincere efforts to work cooperatively with its allies. During the Cold War, the global nature of this ideological conflict required constant support from US partners. As demonstrated by the Coalition Forces that defeated Iraq in the First Gulf War and the UN's sanctions against that nation, the Bush and Clinton Administrations worked closely with and had good relations with American allies. While the United States was the dominant power in these alliances, previous administrations made sure to consult with its allies and follow their recommendations as much as possible. Bush and his advisor believed that dependence on multilateralism would hinder the nation from quickly addressing dangerous situations. The Administration's unilateral approach concluded these arrangements were beneficial, but when it was necessary, the United States would act alone to secure its objectives.

The primary goal that was identified by the Bush Doctrine was American global hegemony. The Administration believed that the United States must ensure an overwhelming dominance in the world because of the absence of globally recognized rules and norms. As a result, the United States must increase its military superiority and use this to maintain security and, global stability, and the spread of American values. To ensure that American military dominance would be unchallenged, the Administration needed to increase military spending. In 2000, military spending equaled $290.6 billion, but within a year it surpassed $308 billion and reached to $606.5 billion by 2008.[26]

The advocates of the Bush Doctrine supported new foreign policy initiatives because of their worldview. The existence of weapons of mass destruction, rogue nations, and radical and violent terrorist groups made the old containment policy inadequate and demanded the changes advocated by the Bush Administration. The critics of this policy argued that the objective of securing American hegemony required a massive military budget, preemptive strikes, and unilateralism, and would lead to the overextension of American resources, and weaken alliances.

CONCLUSION

The Roosevelt Corollary to the Monroe Doctrine and the Bush Doctrine had a significant impact on the direction of American foreign policy. After reading both documents as well as this essay, you should be able to identify many similarities in both the events leading up to the implementation of the Roosevelt Corollary and the Bush Doctrine as well as the key elements of their foreign policy initiatives. This begs the question, how would Roosevelt have acted if he was President in 2001? Would he support the dramatic changes outlined in the Bush Doctrine?

QUESTIONS FOR FURTHER DISCUSSION

- What were the key events that led Roosevelt to pen the Roosevelt Corollary?
- What are the key changes advocated by Roosevelt?
- How did he justify these changes?
- How would the people of Latin America view the Roosevelt Corollary?
- What were the key events that led to the implementation of the Bush Doctrine?
- What are the key points in Bush's commencement address?
- How was Bush's view of the world monolithic?
- How might people in other parts of the world view the Bush Doctrine?
- What are the similarities and differences between the two speeches?
- What are the similarities and differences between the Roosevelt Corollary and the Bush Doctrine?
- How do you think Roosevelt would have viewed the Bush Doctrine?

NOTES

1. Matthias Mass, "Catalyst for the Roosevelt Corollary: Arbitrating the 1902–1903 Venezuelan Crisis and Its Impact on the Development of the Roosevelt Corollary to the Monroe Doctrine," *Diplomacy and Statecraft* 20 (2009): 384.

2. Kris James Mitchener and Marc Weidenmier, "Empire of Public Goods and the Roosevelt Corollary," *The Journal of Economic History* 65, No. 3 (September, 2005): 660–667.

3. Mark T. Gilderhus, "Bravado and Bluster: TR's Sphere of Influence in the Caribbean," in *Major Problems in American Foreign Relations*, 6th ed. edited by Dennis Merrill and Thomas G. Paterson (New York: Houghton Mifflin, 2005): 407.

4. Serge Ricard, "The Roosevelt Corollary," *Presidential Studies Quarterly*, 36 (March, 2006): 20.

5. Mitchener and Weidenmier, "Empire of Public Goods and the Roosevelt Corollary," 660–667.

6. Mass, "Catalyst for the Roosevelt Corollary," 385; Ricard, "The Roosevelt Corollary," 24.

7. Kevin Anderson, "The Venezuelan Claims, Controversy at the Hague, 1903." *The Historian*, 77: (Spring 1995): 528.

8. Mitchener and Weidenmier, "Empire of Public Goods and the Roosevelt Corollary," 662–669.

9. Edward Rhodes, *Presence, Prevention, and Persuasion, A Historical Analysis of Military Force, and Political Influence* (New York: Lexington Books, 2003): 177.

10. Mitchener and Weidenmier, "Empire and Public Good," 20–21; Harold Eugene Davis, John J. Finan, F. Taylor Peck, *Latin American Diplomatic History, An Introduction* (Baton Rouge, Louisiana State University Press, 1977): 154–155.

11. Gilderhus, "Bravado and Bluster," 408; Walter LaFeber, *The New Empire*: *An Interpretation of American Expansion 1860–1898* (Itaca, Cornell University Press, 1963): 182–185.

12. Gilderhus, "Bravado and Bluster," 410–411.

13. John A. Crow, *The Epic of Latin America*, 4th ed. (Berkeley: University of California Press, 1992): 686–687.

14. Shah M. Tarzi, "The Folly of a Grand Strategy of Coercive Global Primacy: A Fresh Perspective on the Post-9/11 Bush Doctrine." *International Journal of World Peace*, XXXI NO. 3 (September 2014): 27–28.

15. Maria Helena De Castro Santos and Ullsses Tavares Teixeira, "The Essential Role of Democracy in the Bush Doctrine: the Invasion of Iraq and Afghanistan," *Revista Brasileira de Política Internacional* 56 Issue 2 (2013): 133–134.

16. Evan Thomas, John Evan, Michael Isikoff, Richard Wolffe, Michael Hirsh, Christopher Dickey, "The 12 Year Itch," *Newsweek*, March 31, 2003. http://eds.b.ebscohost.com. libdb.dccc.edu/eds/detail/detail?sid=4c0927e2-c9ed-4285-8463-c3491e903a8d%40session mgr107&vid=4&hid=117&bdata=JnNpdGU9ZWRzLWxpdmU%3d#AN=9359118&db=f5h; "Analysis: America's New Approach to the World," *Front Line*. http://www.pbs.org/wgbh/pages/frontline/shows/iraq/themes.

17. Stephen Zunes, "Continuing Storm: The U.S. Role in the Middle East." Foreign Policy in Focus, April 1, 1991. http://fpif.org/continuing_storm_the_us_role_in_the_middle_east/; David Rieff, Were Sanctions Right, *New York Times Magazine*, July 27, 2003. http://www.nytimes.com/2003/07/27/magazine/were-sanctions-right.html.

18. It should also be noted that the survival of the Hussein Regime was a factor in the decision to maintain American bases in Saudi Arabia, and the presence of American troops in the Islamic Holy Land was one of Osama bin Laden's reasons for his war against the United States.

19. "Excerpts From Pentagon's Plan: 'Prevent the Re-Emergence of a New Rival'" *New York Times*, March 8 1992. http://www.nytimes.com/1992/03/08/world/excerpts-from-pentagon-s-plan-prevent-the-re-emergence-of-a-new-rival.html?pagewanted=all.

20. The purpose of this leak was to elicit a public debate on Wolfowitz' recommendations.

21. Santos and Teixeira, "The Essential Role of Democracy in the Bush Doctrine," 140–141.

22. Robert Jervis, "Understanding the Bush Doctrine," *Political Science Quarterly*, 118 no. 3 (2003): 368.

23. Non-state actors are entities that influence global politics but are not tied to a particular nation.

24. Jeffrey Record, "The Bush Doctrine and the War in Iraq," *Parameters* (Spring 2003), 4; Jarvis, "Understanding the Bush Doctrine," 369–372.

25. Record, "The Bush Doctrine and the War in Iraq," 4.

26. Santos and Teixeira, "The Essential Role of Democracy in the Bush Doctrine," 140–141.

Operation Eagle Claw: The United States' First Counterterrorist Operation

Jeffrey LaMonica

> Late yesterday, I cancelled a carefully planned operation which was underway in Iran to position our rescue team for later withdrawal of American hostages, who have been held captive there since November 4. Equipment failure in the rescue helicopters made it necessary to end the mission . . . This rescue attempt had to await my judgment that the Iranian authorities could not or would not resolve this crisis on their own initiative . . . It was my decision to attempt the rescue operation. It was my decision to cancel it when problems developed in the placement of our rescue team . . . The responsibility is fully my own.
>
> —President Jimmy Carter, *Statement on the Iran Rescue Mission*, 1980

INTRODUCTION

The failure of Operation Eagle Claw, the mission to rescue American hostages in Iran in April 1980, was the darkest day of Jimmy Carter's presidency. It also represented the United States' first modern counterterrorist operation. Had the mission succeeded, it would have liberated the hostages 230 days earlier than their 20 January 1981 release date. The United States would have made a non-negotiable "zero tolerance" statement to terrorists around the world. The operation would have served as a model for future American counterterrorist operations. Unfortunately, weather, bad luck, mechanical failure, and human error caused the mission to end in tragedy and fade into obscurity.

Nevertheless, Operation Eagle Claw marks a watershed moment in the evolution of United States counterterrorist warfare.

HOSTAGE CRISIS IN IRAN

Iranian terrorists seized the United States Embassy in Teheran, Iran, and took fifty-two Americans captive on 4 November 1979. In the following months, there was bitter disagreement within the Carter Administration over whether or not the situation required military action. United States Secretary of State Cyrus Vance opposed using military force in Iran. He thought persistent and carefully planned negotiations with the terrorists would eventually bring the hostages home. Vance did not believe the terrorists intended to harm the captives. He argued that a rescue raid would place the hostages in unnecessary danger. Furthermore, the Secretary of State asserted that a military operation against Iran would turn other Middle Eastern countries against the United States and threaten American oil interests in the Persian

Statue of President Carter in Atlanta, Georgia

Gulf. After protesting against a rescue mission for nearly six months, Vance resigned as secretary of state just before Operation Eagle Claw launched in April 1980.[1]

President Carter's National Security Advisor Zbigniew Brzezinski wanted to take a hardline stance on the situation in Iran. He was an ardent proponent of a military rescue mission. Brzezinski urged Carter to authorize a raid in accordance with four guidelines; plan in secret, utilize a small military taskforce, protect the lives of the hostages at all costs, and keep Iranian casualties to a minimum. Meanwhile, White House Chief of Staff Hamilton Jordan hoped that diplomatic maneuvering between the United States, the Iranian Government, and the terrorists could attain the release of the captives. Although the connection between the terrorists and the Iranian Government remained obscure, Jordan conducted several negotiations with Iranian politicians he believed had influence over the terrorists. In his last meeting with representatives from Iran on 18 April, Jordan learned that the Iranian Government did not intend to address the release of the American hostages until after their parliamentary elections in mid-May. When Jordan's effort to achieve a diplomatic resolution stalled, President Carter authorized Operation Eagle Claw on 23 April. He made a fateful pledge to accept full responsibility if the mission failed.[2]

PLANNING THE MISSION

The United States Joint Chiefs of Staff considered several possible rescue options. For example, one proposal involved dropping paratroopers into Iran. Another called for sending a small mechanized force into Iran across the Turkish border. The chances of misdropping paratroopers in the Iranian desert were too high in the airborne scenario and the numerous vehicle checkpoints along the Turkish-Iranian border made a motorized invasion too risky. Needless to say, the Joint Chiefs soon abandoned these proposals.[3]

The Joint Chiefs eventually settled on Operation Eagle Claw. The plan involved eight US Navy Sea Stallion helicopters inserting the First Special Forces Operational Detachment-Delta (Delta Force) directly into Iran under cover of night. The helicopters would depart from the aircraft carrier *USS Nimitz* in the Gulf of Oman, refuel at an isolated area of the Iranian desert (codenamed Desert One), and drop Delta Force at a *wadi* fifty miles outside of Teheran (codenamed Desert Two). Six trucks, driven by Central Intelligence Agency personnel already in Iran, would carry Delta Force to the embassy in Tehran. Delta Force would blow a hole in the east wall of the embassy compound. Two forty-man assault groups would enter the embassy, free the hostages, neutralize any terrorist resistance, and escort the captives to the nearby Amjadieh Soccer Stadium for helicopter extraction to Manzariyeh Airstrip. Two C-141 Star Lifters at Manzariyeh would then carry the taskforce and the hostages out of Iran. Finally, four AC-130 gunships would fly over Tehran and destroy the embassy compound and the abandoned Navy helicopters at Manzarayeh. The raid was supposed to take approximately forty-five minutes.[4]

CATASTROPHE AT DESERT ONE

Unfortunately, Operation Eagle Claw never reached Teheran. The first problems occurred during the night of 24 April when a civilian fuel truck and a passenger bus stumbled upon the taskforce's "isolated" refueling point at Desert One. Delta Force destroyed the fuel truck with an anti-tank rocket, but the resulting conflagration lit up the night sky. The taskforce disabled the bus with small arms fire and detained its forty-three Iranian passengers in the desert.[5]

The situation worsened in the early morning of 25 April when a sandstorm forced the eight helicopters from the *Nimitz* to fall an hour behind schedule. The excessive sand and dust then caused three of the helicopters to breakdown. President Carter had already decided to abort the mission due to the lack of serviceable helicopters when an accident occurred during the refueling process at Desert One. A helicopter rotor struck a grounded transport aircraft causing a massive explosion that killed eight Americans and wounded five others. The rest of the taskforce evacuated, leaving the dead servicemen and four helicopters in the Iranian desert.[6]

AFTERMATH AND LEGACY

An investigation committee, led by Admiral James L. Holloway, analyzed the failure of Operation Eagle Claw in August 1980. The committee criticized the taskforce's piecemeal preparation for the raid. Delta Force trained at the Yuma Proving Grounds in Arizona, the US Navy helicopter crews rehearsed at the Naval Air Station in Norfolk, Virginia, the C-141 pilots prepared in Nevada, and the C-130 crews practiced over the Pacific Ocean. The Holloway Committee determined that a joint combined-arms

Anti-American graffiti on the wall of the former US Embassy in Teheran, Iran

training program would have made for better cohesion between the taskforce components and improved their ability to improvise in response to the accident at Desert One.[7]

The committee decided that the number of helicopters used for the mission was not sufficient. Eight helicopters left too narrow a margin for error when the sandstorm disabled three of them. The Holloway Committee also declared the operation's weather reconnaissance inadequate, impeding the taskforce's ability to foresee the sandstorm at the outset. The committee criticized the taskforce planners for not allowing a C-130 Pathfinder with meteorological equipment to fly ahead of the helicopters as they made their way across the Iranian desert. This would have allowed the taskforce to alter or abort the mission due to poor visibility.[8]

Despite the failure of Operation Eagle Claw and the resulting criticism, the United States took its first step in a new era of counterterrorist warfare. Most major European powers had already faced some form of terrorism since the end of the Second World War. The United States was simply not primed for a terrorist challenge in 1979. For example, the Pentagon had only formed Delta Force two years earlier.

The US Government examined the state of its counterterrorist capabilities after the disaster at Desert One. The Senate Armed Services Committee consulted with Delta Force Commander Colonel Charles A. Beckwith about the lessons learned from Operation Eagle Claw. He recommended developing standard tactics and training for all American counterterrorist forces and creating a permanent joint special operations command. Furthermore, Beckwith made a case for establishing forward staging areas for US counterterrorist operations around the world to allow for faster and more efficient deployment.[9] Based on these suggestions, Congress formed the Joint Special Operations Command (JSOC) on 15 December 1980 to prepare all US armed forces for low intensity conflicts and counterterrorism. Congress created the position of Assistant Secretary of Defense for Special Operations and Low Intensity Conflict in 1987. The creation of this office guaranteed regular funding and standardized tactics and training for counterterrorist forces across all branches of the US military.[10] The tragic lessons learned from Operation Eagle Claw ensured that United States would never find itself completely unprepared for a hostage crisis in the future.

QUESTIONS FOR FURTHER DISCUSSION

- Do Special Forces Operations, such as Delta Force, represent a more effective method for waging war against terrorism than conventional military forces?

- Considering the divisions within the Carter Administration over how to deal with the Iranian Hostage Crisis, what are the advantages and disadvantages of attempting to negotiate with terrorists?

NOTES

1. Charles A. Beckwith and Donald Knox, *Delta Force: The Army's Elite Counterterrorist Unit* (New York: Avon Books, 1983), 7; James Kyle and John Eidson, *The Guts to Try: The Untold Story of the Iran Hostage Rescue Mission by the On-Scene Desert Commander* (New York: Orion Books, 1990), 186; Cyrus Vance, *Hard Choices: Critical Years in America's Foreign Policy* (New York: Simon and Schuster, 1983), 377.

2. Jimmy Carter, *Keeping Faith: Memoirs of a President* (Fayetteville, AK: University of Arkansas Press, 1982), 516, 520; Hamilton Jordan, *Crisis: The Last Year of the Carter Presidency* (New York: Putnam, 1982), 253; C. E. Holzworth, *Operation Eagle Claw: A Catalyst for Change in the American Military*, http://www.globalsecurity.org/miltary/library/report/1997/Holzworth.htm.

3. United States Joint Chiefs of Staff Special Operations Review Group, Rescue Mission Report (August 1980), http://nsarchive.gwu.edu/NSAEBB/NSAEBB63/doc8.pdf; Beckwith and Knox, 239; Holzworth.

4. Beckwith and Knox, 5, 280; Charles Cogan, "Desert One and Its Disorders," *The Journal of Military History* 67 (2003): 210.

5. Carter, 520.

6. United States Joint Chiefs of Staff Special Operations Review Group; Beckwith and Knox, 263; Kyle and Eidson, 179.

7. Beckwith and Knox, 273; Kyle and Eidson, 71.

8. United States Joint Chiefs of Staff Special Operations Review Group; Kyle and Eidson, 178.

9. Beckwith and Knox, 326.

10. Matthew Johnson, "The Growing Relevance of Special Operations Forces in US Military Strategy," *Comparative Strategy* 25 (2006): 280.

BIBLIOGRAPHY/SUGGESTED READINGS

Primary Sources

United States Joint Chiefs of Staff Special Operations Review Group, *Rescue Mission Report*. (August 1980). Accessed June 20, 2016. http://nsarchive.gwu.edu/NSAEBB/NSAEBB63/doc8.pdf

Books

Beckwith, Charles A. and Donald Knox. *Delta Force: The Army's Elite Counterterrorist Unit*. New York: Avon Books, 1983.

Carter, Jimmy. *Keeping Faith: Memoirs of a President*. Fayetteville, AK: University of Arkansas Press, 1982.

Jordan, Hamilton. *Crisis: The Last Year of the Carter Presidency*. New York: Putnam, 1982.

Kyle, James and John Eidson. *The Guts to Try: The Untold Story of the Iran Hostage Rescue Mission by the On-Scene Desert Commander*. New York: Orion Books, 1990.

Vance, Cyrus. *Hard Choices: Critical Years in America's Foreign Policy*. New York: Simon and Schuster, 1983.

Articles

Cogan, Charles. "Desert One and Its Disorders." *The Journal of Military History* 67 (2003): 201–16.

Johnson, Matthew. "The Growing Relevance of Special Operations Forces in US Military Strategy." *Comparative Strategy* 25 (2006): 273–96.

Online Sources

Holzworth, C. E. *Operation Eagle Claw: A Catalyst for Change in the American Military*. (1997) Accessed June 20, 2016. http://www.globalsecurity.org/miltary/library/report/1997/Holzworth.htm

The Black Sea Crisis, 2014–15

Jeffrey LaMonica

A referendum was held in Crimea on March 16 in full compliance with democratic procedures and international norms. More than 82 percent of the electorate took part in the vote. Over 96 percent of them spoke out in favor of reuniting with Russia. These numbers speak for themselves. To understand the reason behind such a choice it is enough to know the history of Crimea and what Russia and Crimea have always meant for each other.

—Vladimir Putin, 2014

We do not and will not recognize Russia's illegal and illegitimate 'annexation' of Crimea. We demand that Russia comply with international law and its international obligations and responsibilities; end its illegitimate occupation of Crimea; refrain from aggressive actions against Ukraine; withdraw its troops; halt the flow of weapons, equipment, people and money across the border to the separatists; and stop fomenting tension along and across the Ukrainian border.

—NATO, *Wales Summit Declaration*, 2014

INTRODUCTION

Crimea voted to secede from Ukraine and join the Russian Federation on 16 March 2014. Eighty-two percent of the Crimean population participated in the vote. Ninety-six percent of the voters favored secession. Russian Federation President Vladimir Putin approved the annexation of Crimea based upon the will of the Crimean people and a poll showing ninety-two percent of Russians supporting unification.[1] The European Union (EU), the United States, and the North Atlantic Treaty Organization (NATO) refused to recognize neither Crimea's secession from Ukraine nor Russia's annexation of the peninsula, claiming both to be violations of international law.

Later that March, a civil war erupted in eastern Ukraine when pro-Russian, separatist, paramilitary forces, seeking to create a "New Russia" in eastern Ukraine, clashed with Ukrainian anti-separatist militia. The Ukrainian government and military supported the anti-separatists, but remained largely caught in the middle of the civil conflict. President Putin immediately began supporting the separatists by sending Russian "aid convoys" across the Russo/Ukrainian border to eastern Ukraine. Putin considered the "New Russia" movement to be an extension of the Crimean secession and pledged his country's support for the self-determination of Russians living in Ukraine. The EU and NATO questioned the purpose and content of Putin's "aid convoys" and accused Russia of supplying the separatists with military aid. By April, the EU demanded that Putin halt the "aid convoys," called for multilateral negotiations to settle the civil war in eastern Ukraine, and began sanctioning the Russian Federation.

Petro Poroshenko became the elected president of Ukraine in May 2014 and negotiated a ceasefire in eastern Ukraine the following month. Paramilitary violence broke Poroshenko's armistice in July and reignited the civil war in eastern Ukraine. To make matters worse, an anti-aircraft missile brought down Malaysia Airlines Flight MH17 over eastern Ukraine on 17 July killing 298 civilian passengers. Neither side accepted responsibility for shooting down the airliner, but the missile's Russian origin seemed to implicate the separatists. In response to the tragedy, the EU increased its sanctions against the Russian Federation and began sanctioning Crimea as well. EU concerns in the Black Sea region intensified in fall 2014 with reports of human rights violations against Crimea's Turkish Tatar minority and "unmarked" armored military vehicles

Ukrainian President Petro Poroshenko

crossing the Russo/Ukraine border into eastern Ukraine. The EU extended all sanctions on Russia and Crimea until 2016.[2]

NATO'S POSITION ON UKRAINE

The North Atlantic Treaty Organization issued its *Wales Summit Declaration* in September 2014. The document accused Russia of disrupting freedom and peace in Crimea and eastern Ukraine. "We do not and will not recognize Russia's illegal and illegitimate 'annexation' of Crimea." It condemned Russia's actions as a coercive show of force and recommended that national boundaries in the region be resolved through politics and diplomacy. NATO proclaimed its commitment to defend all existing territorial sovereignty in the Black Sea region. The declaration demanded that Russia withdraw its military forces from inside eastern Ukraine and along the Russo/Ukrainian border. It called upon Russia to stop its "aid convoys" from carrying arms, troops, and money to the separatist forces in eastern Ukraine. NATO demanded that "Those directly and indirectly responsible for the downing of MH17 should be held accountable and brought to justice as soon as possible." The document held Russia responsible for protecting the rights and well-being of the Tatar minority in Crimea. The declaration also outlined NATO's plan for crisis management in the region. It placed NATO's Northeast Headquarters in Latvia in a state of readiness, initiated military training maneuvers aimed at disarming paramilitary forces, and increased NATO's overall defense budget. Finally, the document pledged NATO's support for all EU sanctions against Russia and Crimea.[3]

THE EU'S POSITION ON UKRAINE

The European Union has been taking steps toward admitting Ukraine into its ranks since late 2012. Before the outbreak of civil war in 2014, the EU presided over a natural gas agreement between Ukraine and Russia and monitored Ukraine's treatment of its Tatar minority. The majority of Ukrainians seemed to be supportive of joining the EU prior to the crisis in eastern Ukraine.[4]

After Russia's annexation of Crimea and the outbreak of civil war in eastern Ukraine, the EU implored Russia to remove its military presence from eastern Ukraine and called for multilateral talks between Ukraine, Russia, and Crimea. The EU increased its pressure by cancelling all scheduled talks with Russia, relocating the 2014 Group of Eight summit from Sochi, Russia to Brussels, Belgium, and temporarily excluding Russia from the G8.[5]

The EU recognized the election of Petro Poroshenko as president of Ukraine in May 2014 and endorsed his ceasefire in June. Between August 2014 and January 2015, the EU issued several directives pertaining to the regional crisis, including additional requests for multilateral talks, expressing concerns over the rights of Crimean Tatars, inquiries into Russian troops, weapons, and vehicles crossing into eastern Ukraine, and an offer to send a security mission to peacefully disarm paramilitary groups in eastern Ukraine. None of these EU efforts to mediate or intervene materialized. Nevertheless, the EU kept all sanctions against Russia and Crimea in place. EU sanctions and aid concerning the Black Sea crisis were as follows:

- Suspension of any new financial operations in Russia by the European Investment Bank

- Freezing of assets and suspension of visas of nearly two hundred Russian individuals and "entities" suspected of contributing to the violence in Ukraine

- Ban on loans to five major Russian banks

- Arms embargo against Russia

- Embargo against Russia on services necessary to drilling and producing oil

- Ban on Crimean imports

- Ban on investments in Crimea

- Ban on tourism in Crimea

- Embargo on oil, gas, and mineral exports to Crimea

- Ban on technical assistance regarding infrastructure in Crimea

- Nearly 140 million euros in aid to Ukraine

- Donation of over sixty military vehicles to the Ukrainian Army[6]

PRESIDENT PUTIN'S POSITION ON UKRAINE

Russian Federation President Vladimir Putin addressed the Russian Federal Council and State Duma in March 2014 after Crimea's secession from Ukraine. In addition to attesting to the legality and legitimacy of the Crimean referendum, Putin spoke at length about the shared history and culture of Russia and Crimea as justification for annexation. According to Putin, 1.5 million of Crimea's 2 million residents identify as ethnic Russians. He claimed that Ukraine's break from the Soviet Union in 1991 was against the will of these Crimean Russians and that Russia only reluctantly ceded Crimea to Ukraine in hopes that the Ukrainian Government would protect the rights of Russians living there. Putin accused the Ukrainian Government of failing to maintain the well-being of its Russian inhabitants. Over twenty years of economic depression, political instability, and civil war in Ukraine have forced hundreds of thousands of Crimean Russians across the Russo/Ukrainian border in search of employment and safety from what Putin called violent "Neo-Nazis" and "Russophobes." Furthermore, the Ukrainian Government violated the rights of Crimean Russians when it banned the Russian language in the early 2000s. According to Putin, Russia could no longer stand by and watch the maltreatment of its people by a foreign government.[7]

President Putin disputed EU, US, and NATO accusations of Russia forcefully coercing Crimea to secede from Ukraine. He asserted that Russia has had a legal and consensual military presence in Sevastopol on the Crimean Peninsula since the 1990s and has never used its presence there to influence Ukrainian political affairs. Putin stated that Crimea's decision to secede reflected the will of its overwhelming ethnic Russian majority and the referendum exemplified the United Nation's guidelines for national self-determination. He compared Crimea in 2014 to Kosovo in 2008, "For some reason, things that Kosovo Albanians (and we have full respect for them) were permitted to do, Russians, Ukrainians, and Crimean Tatars in Crimea are not allowed." The President claimed that EU, US, and NATO protests against Russia's annexation of Crimea are born out of their own desires to diminish Russian presence on the Crimean Peninsula, absorb Ukraine into the EU and NATO, and increase their own hegemony in the Black Sea region. Putin alluded to this Western hypocrisy in his speech, "Western Europe and North America? They say we are violating norms of international law. Firstly, it's a good thing that they at least remember that there exists such a thing as international law—better late than never." He clearly stated that any Western attempt to usurp Russian influence in the Black Sea region would be considered a direct threat to the Russian Federation, "Russia is an independent, active participant in international affairs; like other countries, it has its own national interests that need to be taken into account and respected."[8]

President Putin spoke with his Federal Security Service about the civil war in eastern Ukraine in March 2015. He reaffirmed Russia's commitment to establishing peace and stability in the Black Sea region and prosecuting those who perpetuate the crisis in eastern Ukraine. Putin pledged Russia's continued obligation to send "aid convoys" to the pro-Russian separatists and accept refugees from war-torn eastern Ukraine. Furthermore, Putin swore that Crimean Tatars will enjoy the same rights as the numerous Turkish minorities already living in the Russian Federation. Putin concluded his speech by claiming that NATO's increased military presence in central and eastern Europe poses a direct threat to the Russian Federation.[9]

A Russian Naval Vessel in Sevastopol, Crimea

OTHER CONSIDERATIONS

Ethnicity and ideology play a central role in the Black Sea crisis. The origins of these factors go back at least seventy years. Ukraine has suffered from an ethnic and ideological identity crisis since anti-Communist Ukrainians, who did not identify as ethnic Russians, sided with invaders from Nazi Germany against the Soviet Red Army during the Second World War. For these anti-Communist partisans, the war represented a failed opportunity to free Ukraine from the Soviet Union. The collapse of the Soviet Union and Ukrainian independence in 1991 deepened the ethnic and ideological fissures in the region. A major flashpoint came in the early 2000s, when the Ukrainian government attempted to cultivate a sense of Ukrainian identity by banning the Russian language. During the current crisis, the separatists in eastern Ukraine generally identify as ethnic Russians with Marxist/Communist ideology. On the other hand, the anti-separatists usually see themselves as ethnic Ukrainians with right-wing ideology.

POSSIBLE OUTCOMES

The European Union may be able to deescalate the Black Sea crisis by expanding its effort to initiate multilateral talks with presidents Poroshenko and Putin. The EU set aside a mediation budget in 2013 to create a taskforce similar to the United Nations Department of Political Affairs Mediation Standby Team. This team is comprised of experts in constitution writing, human rights, international justice, and global security. The EU would most likely need to launch a peacekeeping operation to disarm paramilitary groups and maintain a ceasefire in eastern Ukraine while this taskforce oversees negotiations. At present, the EU's peacekeeping contingent, the European Union Force, lacks the manpower and resources necessary for a mission of this proportion.

The EU may also force a diplomatic solution by expanding sanctions against Russia. Long-term comprehensive sanctions may prove untenable, however, as several leading EU members depend on trade with Russia, especially Russian natural gas. President Putin has already banned food imports from all EU nations. A Russian embargo on exporting natural gas may be more than some EU members, particularly Germany, can endure.

NATO intervention in eastern Ukraine seems highly unlikely given the complexities it would face in both establishing justification for a military incursion and devising an appropriate strategy for resolving the conflict. Ukraine is not an official NATO ally, its territorial integrity is not guaranteed under the terms of the alliance, nor is any member of NATO obligated to militarily intervene on Ukraine's behalf. Even if Ukraine became a NATO member, without a conventional Russian military invasion of Ukraine, the crisis in eastern Ukraine remains an internal civil war outside the parameters of the alliance. NATO forces would be hard-pressed in deciding which side to support in the civil war. Both separatist and anti-separatist forces conduct illegal paramilitary operations resulting in frequent atrocities against civilians. The best NATO forces could do in eastern Ukraine is join the Ukrainian Army in its already futile attempt to quell paramilitary violence and maintain national unity. This would likely devolve into a military, strategic, and diplomatic quagmire for NATO. Furthermore, President Putin has been very direct in asserting that any NATO involvement in the Black Sea region will be construed as a threat to the Russian Federation. NATO members are not likely to agree on a course of action which could ignite another East/West standoff reminiscent of the Cold War.

In truth, President Putin may be in the best position to restore stability by negotiating a reconfiguration of territorial boundaries in the Black Sea region. The Russian president seems to be more informed than the EU, US, and NATO about the historical and ethnic dynamics of the situation. Thus far, Putin has put forward rational arguments concerning the political and economic failures of Ukraine since 1991, the right to self-determination of ethnic Russians living in Crimea and eastern Ukraine, and Russia's national interests in the Black Sea region. After all, Sevastopol has been home to Russia's Black Sea Fleet for nearly three hundred years. Furthermore, Putin has been quick to remind multinational organizations, such as the EU and NATO, of their poor track record in central and eastern Europe over the last twenty-five years. He has also pointed to Western contradictions in invoking idealistic justifications for self-serving foreign interventions. The Russian president exclaimed in March 2015, "After the dissolution of bipolarity on the planet, we no longer have stability. Key international institutions are not getting any stronger; on the contrary, in many cases, they are sadly degrading. Our western partners, led by the United States of America . . . decide destinies of the world, that only they can ever be right."[10]

QUESTIONS FOR FURTHER DISCUSSION

- Is President Putin, NATO, or the EU in the best position to understand the complexities of the civil war in eastern Ukraine and provide a solution?

- Are economic sanctions a viable and fair way for international organizations, such as the EU, to peacefully coerce the governments of sovereign nations?

NOTES

1. Vladimir Putin, *Address by President of the Russian Federation, 18 March 2014*. Accessed June 10, 2015. (http://en.kremlin.ru/events/president/news/20603).

2. Ibid.

3. NATO, *Wales Summit Declaration, 5 September 2014*. Accessed June 10, 2015. (http://www.nato.int/cps/en/natohq/official_texts_112964.htm).

4. EU, *Factsheet: EU-Ukraine Relations, 18 March 2014*. Accessed June 10, 2015. (http://eu-un.europa.eu/articles/en/article_14756_en.htm).

5. Ibid.

6. Ibid.

7. Vladimir Putin, *Address by President of the Russian Federation, 18 March 2014*.

8. Ibid.

9. Vladimir Putin, *Federal Security Service Board Meeting, 26 March 2015*. Accessed June 10, 2015. (http://en.kremlin.ru/events/president/news/49006).

10. Vladimir Putin, *Federal Security Service Board Meeting, 26 March 2015*.

CPSIA information can be obtained
at www.ICGtesting.com
Printed in the USA
LVOW09s1224301116

515016LV00001B/1/P

9 781524 913106